Getting
Strong
in All
the Hurting
Places

Getting Strong in All the Hurting Places

Phyllis and David York

RAWSON ASSOCIATES

NEW YORK

Copyright © 1989 by Phyllis and David York

Library of Congress Cataloging in Publication Data

York, Phyllis, 1937–
    Getting strong in all the hurting places / by Phyllis and David York.
    ISBN 0-89256-345-1
    1. York, Phyllis, 1937—Health.   2. Quadriplegics—Pennsylvania-
-Biography.   I. York, David, 1929–   . II. Title.
RC406.Q33Y67   1989
362.4'3'092-dc20
[B]   88-43557
                                                                                CIP

Rawson Associates
Macmillan Publishing Company
866 Third Avenue, New York, N.Y. 10022
Collier Macmillan Canada, Inc.

Macmillan books are available at special discounts for bulk purchases for sales
promotions, premiums, fund-raising, or educational use. For details, contact:

                        Special Sales Director
                        Macmillan Publishing Company
                        866 Third Avenue
                        New York, N.Y. 10022

Packaged by Rapid Transcript, a division of March Tenth, Inc.

Designed by Stanley S. Drate/Folio Graphics Co. Inc.

10   9   8   7   6   5   4   3   2   1

Printed in the United States of America

Most names in this book have been changed to protect the privacy of the
individuals involved.

*This book is dedicated to all people in
need of healing.*

From the depths of our hearts we thank
our most loving family, friends, and the
professionals who suffered us.

---— ✳ **I** ✳ ---—

PHYLLIS

✳ Today I broke my neck. The worst part is that I am naked and the ambulance people who are coming to help me are friends and neighbors. I am so embarrassed I want to die. Please kill me.

All I want is to be back in yesterday's early-morning sun, as we awoke entwined in each other's body. My belly is snuggled in the arch of David's back. Soon we are moving against each other, touching, feeling, seeking, loving each other, casual and easy, as though it has always been this good and will stay this good forever.

Later, walking toward the footpath down to the canal that runs along the Delaware, I pass old Pennsylvania houses restored, renovated, redone by tourists like us who have come to settle in this quiet town of Point Pleasant. The houses are at steep angles to the river, seeming to resist its pull. How I love this little place, where neighbors native to the Pennsylvania hillsides welcomed us with boxes of home-grown raspberries and filled us in on their town's heritage. The small grocery in town is stocked to serve the campers who come to spend their days on the river in tubes, canoes, and boats. A runner is passing the Post Office where later people will meet and talk as they thumb the day's mail. The runner gives me a wave and whisks past the Volunteer Fire Department and Ambulance Service Station at the edge of the red wooden bridge leading to the canal. I follow at my own walking pace.

I am trying to be consistent with this early-morning walk. I would like to be more like David, a person who uses routines to make his life easier. Each morning he gets up at the same time, folds the bedding the same way, turns up the heat, washes, dresses, goes downstairs, grinds the coffee beans, heats the water, opens the glass doors to the patio and fills the bird feeder. Back in the kitchen he watches the raspberry finches, the blue jays, and the titmouse attack the sunflower seeds before he finishes the coffee. Sometimes if I am there with him he will turn to me and say things like, "Birds really are direct descendants of dinosaurs," or he will sit and tell me a dream he had a few days ago, or about someone he met on one of his bike rides. He has exercised consistently for the last thirty years.

I am compulsive and not very consistent. I get up and go to bed at all different times. I eat and gorge myself, or fast for days at a time. I work day and night for weeks or hardly at all. If the birds were to rely on me to feed them they would live a very uncertain life.

This is the first time I've been out exercising in two weeks, and I am tired. We have been on a book tour for the paperback edition of our very successful hardcover book, *Toughlove*. Yesterday we came home from Cleveland and in two days we leave to do a Toughlove workshop in California. It's funny how a personal tragedy—our own kids being in trouble with drugs and failing school—and our inadequacies in raising our three teenage girls led us to discover methods to help other families in trouble. In certain circles we have become heroes.

The canal is a visual pleasure that allows exercise to be bearable. On this October day the grass is wet, the trees just starting to turn. Hydrangeas in people's yards are still blue but moving toward the rust they will become in late fall.

My destination is five miles down the river where this section of the canal ends in the tiny town of Centerbridge and a telephone booth sits outside Dilly's ice cream stand. I call David to pick me up. "Hi, it's me, you ready?"

"Yup. I'm just putting the cleaning in the car." In a few minutes we're on our way to New Hope for lunch.

"How was the walk?"

"Hard, but I saw a blue heron standing in the canal. Did you see it?" David is the most eagle-eyed person. He is always the first to see a budding forsythia or pussy willow in the early spring. As we drive along he points out hawks and sees fleet-footed deer moving through the forest; he amazes me.

"I didn't see him."

"Maybe when we come back he'll be there."

In ten minutes we are looking out the window of the Havana restaurant. We watch the last of the strolling tourists who pack the streets of New Hope in the summer and linger on in fall, eating ice cream, browsing in the shops. How comfortable we feel here, where restaurant owners and keepers know us well and have become our friends. Jimmy and Jane, Havana's owners, come out to say hello. "We saw you on Donahue. You guys were great. David, I couldn't believe you kept telling Donahue to be quiet."

"Well, we wanted to make our point. We were a lot less intimidated this time. I guess having media experience has helped."

"David, what are you having?" I have to ask because menu anxiety has set in and I want to order everything. David always knows what he is having, and anyway I don't want to order the same thing because there would be less to taste.

"You tell me first," he teases and laughs, and tells me. Finally I make up my mind. "Phyllis, I thought of a really good way to end our new book," and we are off discussing *Toughlove Solutions.*

After we drop off our mountain of cleaning we head home the long way so we can ride through the hills and catch the last of the summer greenery. Driving by the canal, David spots the heron. We park and watch it standing still in the water.

At home the contractor is measuring the living room for bookshelves and working with the designer on the lighting tracks. The renovations on the house should be finished in a few weeks. The new, almost completed kitchen and dining room/work area look great. The upstairs still looks like the wreck of the *Hesperus,* especially with all the packing and unpacking going on.

David is standing at the bedroom door where I have begun to take out clothes for our next week on the road. "Phyllis, we need to talk about the management of Toughlove and our conflict with Art. We need to make a plan. There's about a thousand groups out there and it's costing us a fortune in referral services. We've got to find funding. I'm going to go for a bike ride and think about it."

It is almost dark when David returns. "I was getting worried about you."

"I was tired so I took my time and stopped to rest."

"I've packed most of my stuff and tomorrow we'll fight through yours." We both laugh because I am meticulous about colors and David has no color sense and doesn't care much. We eat, watch TV and kiss each other goodnight.

DAVID

❋ **I**n the early morning, I hear a bumping sound and a sleep-shattering cry, "David! David!"

Oh, God, I think as I rush to the stairway, what if Phyllis has broken an arm or a leg. How will we ever get to finish our *Toughlove* book tour? Phyllis sure picked a bad time to do something dumb.

You look so awkward. Lying on your back, your legs folded over you, your head jammed in the corner. You know right away what has happened. "Oh, my poor darling, I've ruined our life. My neck is broken. I just saw a bright flash, and then pins and needles all over my body."

I am running up and down the stairs, panicked. You tell me, "Get the phone and call the ambulance."

PHYLLIS

❋ **I** cannot move. My whole body is in pain, but flashing

through my mind are childhood images. I am back in the Bronx with Mrs. Hitler, the name we had for the lady who lived and screamed on the top floor of her apartment building. We loved to provoke her by yelling up to her, "Crazy, crazy, crazy, Mrs. Hitler," while jumping up and down on cars parked in the street. Mrs. Hitler would throw water at us, screaming, "Bastards, no goodniks, all goyim. You should drop dead, go to hell." The adults whispered that it was the "change" or her rotten kids that never visited that made her crazy. They didn't seem to notice that we spurred her on.

One night Mrs. Hitler screamed and yelled obscenities in Yiddish and English and the next day the police and men in white coats came to take her away. All of us children stood around the stoop watching as the men pushed and pulled her. Mrs. Hitler was in her nightgown crying and trying to pull her hands free. She kept saying, "Oy, oy, Gott in himmel. I don't go out without my clothes. Please let me cover up."

Fate reached across the years to pay me back. David, I am so embarrassed, I want to die.

DAVID

✳ While we wait, I try to comfort you. "Can you move anything yet? Don't worry, it's just a temporary loss. You didn't fall far enough. You probably have a bad strain. You will be okay once the ambulance gets here. The hospital will set things right, my darling."

I am worried that you may go into shock. You should be covered and kept warm just in case. The problem is that anything I put over you will push your legs down on your chest even further and you're having difficulty breathing now. I am fearful of moving you and terrified of not moving you. Christ! I don't know what to do. Where the hell are those damned ambulance people? Ambulance people, oh my God! If they arrive and see you naked with your legs over your head you will die of embarrassment. I can't leave you like this. I slowly and carefully move your legs and cover you with a blanket. I know it will be all right. After all, you aren't really hurt that badly and shock and embarrassment are deadly. You seem more comfortable now but your breathing is still labored. I hope that what I did was all right. What is keeping that ambulance?

I keep thinking about what I should have done to stop you from falling. I was conscious of your getting out of bed. Why didn't I ask if you were okay? We are remodeling the house and I meant to block the newly placed stairway. I meant to put a night light on in the hall where the steps are.

At last the flashing yellow lights announce the ambulance's arrival and I quickly let the crew in. They are wonderful. The woman in charge tells me, "We're not sure what kind of injury Phyllis has sustained, but just in case, we're making sure that her neck and back are moved as little as possible. We don't want to risk causing even more damage. We'll put a collar on Phyllis's neck and we have to put a board under her to lift her. She's in such a confined space it's going to take time." Turning to Phyllis she says, "How are you feeling, Phyllis? Are you in any pain? Does it hurt in any specific place?"

"No, I don't feel any pain; it's like I have pins and needles all over me, and I'm burning from my shoulders down."

"Okay, it's going to take us some time but we'll get you out of here as quickly as we can."

I sit at the top of the stairs watching. Staying out of the way, while strangers minister to you. After a long, cautious hour you are lifted and carried to the door and you say in a barely audible whisper, "David dearest, call someone to support you."

Asking for help, asking for help! Jesus, how I hate to do it. While driving to some unknown place I would rather muddle around and be lost than stop at a gas station and ask for directions. Each time Phyllis suggests getting directions I furiously tighten my resolve to do it myself. But I can't play the macho jackass now. I decide to call Alan and Gwen. They are two friends who had just vacationed with us in England and we had all gone shark-fishing a week ago. Alan is our dentist and Gwen has been working for Toughlove for several years.

The phone rings and finally stops as the receiver is lifted off the hook. A pause that seems forever is broken when Alan says, "Hello."

"Hello, Alan, this is David. There's been an accident and I need someone to support me."

"Wait a minute, wait a minute. Who's had an accident?"

"Oh, Christ, Phyllis fell down the stairs and they're taking her to the hospital. I'm going there now, can you meet me?"

"Okay, take it slow. First of all, what kind of injury are we talking about?"

"I don't know. The ambulance people are treating her like she broke her neck."

"Okay, what hospital are they taking her to? Is it one in Philadelphia or Smith Hospital in New Hope?"

"Smith Hospital."

"Okay, I'll meet you there as soon as I can."

I hang up the phone relieved. Phyllis's wisdom about me is, as usual, correct. Stuffing down my fear, I leave the house to face our neighbors in the chilly dawn. With jackets and sweaters over their pajamas, they watch. You in your ambulance. Me in my car. Lives in transformation.

II

PHYLLIS

✳ I have pins and needles all over my body. I told the doctor at the local hospital that I don't want to live if I am paralyzed. He said, "It's to early to tell yet." Please, God, kill me before he tells me. Again, thoughts of the past drift through my head to that day when the cemetery was gray, gray, gray. The March sky was winter gray and the ice plants over my beloved grandparents' graves were green gray. The old gray men in their long dirty black coats and hats were rubbing their hands around the black prayer books and taking green money to say a prayer or two for your dead.

The gray shadows over my soul were put there many years ago. My mother, torn between her allegiance to the living and to the dead, pressed my shoulders toward the graves of the beloved Baba and Zada of my childhood and demanded that I ask forgiveness of them for the sins I had committed. The sins of pregnancy and marriage to an outsider, a gentile, a goy.

That day I knew I should be dead.

DAVID

✳ Alan arrives at the local hospital shortly after me. He is a heavy man with a dark beard and hair to match. He has a lust for life that is bigger than he is. Whenever he can, he escapes from the confines of his dental practice to play, which for Alan means hunting, fishing, and training dogs. On our trip to England, Gwen and Phyllis had stayed in London to shop while Alan and I had gone fishing in Scotland. The adventure had allowed us to develop the peculiar male bonding men get when they share adventures.

I pace back and forth in a small waiting room, filled with empty chairs that stare at me. Alan paces with me, talking, asking questions: "What happened? Have you talked to the doctor yet? Let's go get the doctor and find out what we can." Alan forces me out of my deadness. He makes me think about the decisions I hope to avoid.

I need his strength and assertiveness, I can't be passive as I was when Phyllis was hurt in a car accident about ten years ago. The car she was riding in slid on the ice and hit a telephone pole. I rushed to the hospital unsure of what injuries had occurred or how serious they were. I only knew she was in the emergency room. When I arrived the nurse told me Phyllis was in one of the curtained rooms and the doctor was with her. I was told to take a seat and wait. Without thinking or asking how Phyllis was, I did as I was told. Finally a friend came out from behind the curtain and asked me why I was outside instead of being inside with Phyllis. Feeling the fool, I quickly went behind the curtain to see her. Luckily it was only a broken wrist. Maybe we'll be lucky again and this will just be one of those adventures to talk and laugh about.

We find the doctor at the nurses' station drinking coffee.

"I'm Mr. York, Doctor. Can you tell me anything about my wife's injury?"

"I'm sorry, I was about to send one of the nurses for you. I've just finished looking at the x rays. I can't see any broken bones to cause Mrs. York's symptoms." Relief floods through me. "We really need to take a CAT scan but we don't have the equipment here. I recommend you go to Masonic Hospital in Philadelphia.

It's a teaching hospital and some of the best people in the country are there. You'll need to go by ambulance, though."

"Will you get one, Doctor? I'm going to tell my wife."

My relief fades when I see Phyllis lying so still. She is in a brightly lit room with a nurse standing by.

"Hello, David, my darling," she whispers. "Hello Alan, thank you for coming."

I bend down and softly say to her, "Phyllis, the x ray doesn't show that you broke any bones. The doctor recommends we get a CAT scan though, just to make sure. We have to go by ambulance to Masonic Hospital."

"Oh, David, I'm so frightened. I know I've broken my neck. Please, dear, don't leave me alone."

"Don't worry, my dear. I'll stay by your side."

After careful preparation we board the ambulance for a ride to the big-city hospital. I have to sit in front because an attendant needs to ride in the back with you. I try to talk to you from this position but a conversation requires more energy than you seem to have. I stop trying and sit there. Looking through the rearview mirror I see that Alan is following in his car. Seeing him there eases my panic. I notice that some cars respect our siren, while others use it to make their journey go faster. In one town a policeman responds by moving traffic out of our way. Mundane observations and mundane thoughts. A way out of the fear of Now.

The emergency room is filled with the bleeding and sick, injured and drunk. All of us waiting, waiting. Alan comforts me with his small talk, keeping me from my retreat to fear and self-blame.

A young doctor with tired eyes and a weary stance tells us he is taking you for a CAT scan. His parting comment as he disappears behind the safety of the swinging doors is, "It doesn't look good." My heart plummets as I pace the halls with Alan at my side, talking. I try to escape the grasp of pain and sadness, without success.

I know I must call our three kids. I dread the reality that telling them will force upon me.

The first one I manage to get hold of is Jodi, our youngest daughter. She has beautiful red hair and a beautiful face that lets people know that she is Phyllis's daughter. Jodi had a hard time growing up. We became too involved in making our own careers and left her adolescence to chance. She quit school at sixteen after disasters in both public and private school. Fortunately for all of us, she got a job at a bookstore owned and run by Dale, a woman who became a wonderful friend to all of us. Dale filled in much of the parent role that we were not offering and even supplied a model for sibling interaction with her sister, Susan, who ran the bookstore with her. The worlds of books and adults became an environment filled with mentors and friends. This was a growing-up point for Jodi. She began going to Kripali Yogi ashram and found a spiritual life that we lacked and she needed. Jodi started to support herself and studied for a year to complete her General Education Diploma, which made us pleased and proud of her.

Jodi decided that she wanted to become a single mother when she was twenty-two, and seven months before Phyllis's accident had given birth to our first granddaughter, Nitya. We disliked her choice of single parenthood, believing that Jodi did not realize how difficult raising a child is with two parents, never mind doing it alone. But our anger and resistance gradually left as Nitya became a loving reality and Jodi proved she could manage the choice she had made.

I listen to the ringing of the phone, which is barely audible over the pounding of my heart.

"Hello."

"Hello, Jodi, this is Dad. I have some bad news. Mom fell down the steps and broke her neck." Her scream leaves me hanging onto the phone immobilized. Alan takes over and says, "No, Phyllis is not dead, but very seriously injured." His recital of events revives me and comforts Jodi.

Jodi tells Alan that she will come to the hospital as soon as possible. She may not be able to make it until tomorrow because she has to make arrangements for the baby. Alan says, "Jodi, go to a friend's house. You need that support."

My next call is to Heidi, our middle child. Pretty, blonde, and fun-loving, as a result of my mother's genes. Heidi barely manages to clear five feet tall. "Hello, Heidi, this is Dad. I know it's early but there's been an accident. Mom has fallen down the stairs in our house and may have broken her neck."

"Oh, my God! Where are you? I'm coming to the hospital immediately."

"We're in Masonic Hospital but we don't know anything yet for sure. Why don't you wait until we have more information."

"No, Dad. I'm only twenty minutes away and I need to be by Mom's side. I'm coming down."

"Okay, I'm really glad that you're coming. We are in the emergency room. We'll probably still be here when you arrive."

I find her response heartwarming since we have been at odds over her lifestyle. She and her husband have flitted from job to marginal job, never willing to provide much for their family, just going from one economic crisis to another. We couldn't stand the thought of our two little grandchildren suffering for their parent's lack of responsibility, so we would rush in with the magic of money. Finally, we took our heartstrings out of the picture and said that we would no longer be their economic backstop, that until Heidi settled down we did not want to be involved with them in any way. Our impasse had lasted over six months until three days earlier, when Heidi had a dream that prompted her to call us. As a result of her dream, Heidi had decided that she wanted to create more stability for herself and her two sons, and to be a part of our family.

I am glad she is coming to the hospital. I need the comfort of my family around me now.

Nobody answers at Ilene's number, but I keep calling and calling. Through action I avoid feeling.

PHYLLIS

❊ The local hospital tried to kill me after all. They sent me to the big-city butcher shop. After a wait that seems forever, they wheel me into the x-ray room, where the CAT scan closes in and smothers me. Then I'm left on a table alone in a dimly lit room with the door closed. Unable to move I am disoriented and blackness isolates me. I cry out, "Help! Help!" but no one answers. "David, David, get me out of here fast." Finally an attendant appears and wheels me back to the emergency room. David, Alan, and the doctor are waiting but I am too tired to pay attention to anything.

DAVID

✳ A half-hour after contacting Heidi, a time that seems like an eternity, the doctor invites us back through the swinging doors, past the sacred white curtains to where you lie. I take your hand. The familiar contours, the warmth and softness are still there, but the unfamiliar small weak movements your hand makes are a jarring reminder of how little is left.

"The CAT scan indicates a dislocation of the seventh cervical and first thoracic vertebrae. They are the lowest vertebra in Mrs. York's neck and the first vertebra in the shoulder area," the doctor tells us. "Since no function—that is, increased movement—has occurred, Mrs. York is going to be paralyzed. She is never going to walk again." I try desperately to hear but know I don't understand what has been said.

I am grateful when, again, Alan takes over, "Phyllis looks tired and needs to rest. Can we talk outside?"

The three of us push the curtain aside and walk to the middle of the room. We are surrounded by people being stitched and mended. The doctor repeats his story. "In ninety percent of the cases of spinal cord injury, the return of physical function several hours after the trauma is all that returns. The sooner the patient and family accept that fact, the quicker effective rehabilitation can occur. The next step is to put tongs into Mrs. York's skull and attach forty pounds of weight for traction. Over time the muscles will fatigue from the tension and relax, which will hopefully allow the dislocated vertebrae to slip back into place. If this does not occur in a few days we will operate and manually reset the vertebrae." A calm litany of welcome to the world of the spinal cord injured. Thank God, Alan takes over again, asking the questions that I don't know enough to ask:

"Are you a resident?"

"Yes."

"What year are you in?"

"My first."

"When will your supervisor see Phyllis?"

"Probably Monday."

"Where is the best hospital available for this type of injury?"

"Right here. We are a teaching hospital and the best doctors consult here."

"Is there any other hospital that specializes in spinal cord injuries?"

"Well, Jefferson Hospital does."

"What is the difference between them and you?"

With great reluctance we are informed that Jefferson is the spinal cord trauma center for this area. They have a large Federally funded research program and provide better nursing care.

As Alan questions, I come out of my shock-induced stupor. I can't afford that luxury.

"Okay, we are moving her to Jefferson Hospital." The doctor petulantly puts the bureaucratic wheels into action.

Heidi arrives just as we finish talking to the doctor. She looks anxious and frightened. We both hug each other and Heidi asks, "How are you doing, Dad?"

"I'm okay, pretty scared. We're sure that Mom has broken her neck and we're taking her to Jefferson Hospital; they specialize in spinal cord injury. Mom's over behind that curtain. Go on over and see her. Alan and I will be over in a minute."

$$\text{---} \quad \ast \quad \textbf{III} \quad \ast \quad \text{---}$$

PHYLLIS

❋ Heidi is suddenly standing by my stretcher. Even in this condition I want to protect her, something I did not do well enough through her turbulent teen years.

"Oh, Heidi, I'm so glad to see you. I'll be all right."

"I know, I know," she says. As I fade out I see Alan and David talking to the doctor.

Later David leans over me, "Phyllis, my darling, we're taking you to Jefferson Hospital. It's in Philadelphia, not far from here. They are the spinal cord trauma center and they specialize in spinal cord injury. We need to take one more ambulance drive, dearest. You'll be all right, sweetheart, just hang in there a little while longer."

I am glad to be leaving. My CAT-scan experience has been enough of this hospital for me.

DAVID

❋ Alan and I make sure the ambulance is ordered and then join Heidi. She is standing next to Phyllis, holding her hand with tears streaming down her face. We join her, tears and all, until the ambulance arrives.

How quickly our life has changed. Seven steps, a distance of five feet. That is all. Our trip to California to be on TV and radio has become an ambulance-wailing journey to another hospital and into a new life.

Jefferson Hospital is everything we hoped for. We are met at the door by two nurses and two residents and our friends Gwen and Teresa.

When we met Teresa eight years ago she was volunteering at a drug and alcohol rehabilitation program where Phyllis and I had been hired to start and run a family therapy program. Teresa's daughter, Maureen, had successfully gone through the program and Teresa was grateful, which meant she now had a cause to believe in and devote her time to. She became our assistant and soon switched her fierce loyalty to us. When we started Toughlove, Teresa came with us. Tom, an aluminum siding salesman, seems to be an extension of Teresa. His work allowed him the flexible hours to become the houseperson when their daughter Maureen became bedridden with multiple sclerosis. They have the patience of saints; their care and attention has kept their daughter with them. Last year alone she went into the intensive care unit fifteen times. One of them managed to stay with Maureen twenty-four hours a day. It is as if by sheer willpower they have kept her alive. Each time their daughter was weaker, making her next return to intensive care seem like the last. I don't think I can be as good as they are.

Teresa rushes into the waiting ambulance and kisses you on the cheek before the horrified attendants know what is happening. They all yell, "Get out of the ambulance. You may not touch the patient." They fear the slightest jostle will cause problems as yet unseen, and Teresa's impulsive act catches them unawares. Teresa's care and protection have always been a boon and problem. When we were doing family therapy we often had Teresa sit in with us as a cotherapist. In this way she could be aware of the family issues and work with the rest of the treatment staff in our absence. During one session when Phyllis was helping a family come to grips with a mother's alcoholism, the mother told Phyllis, "You are a stupid, stupid woman." Teresa's reaction was instantaneous, "She is not stupid. Phyllis is the smartest person I know!" Phyllis and the entire family were dumbfounded by this vehement outburst.

Gwen, Alan's wife, always seems subdued in his presence. Heavy and dark like Alan, she has earned her way into the Toughlove organization through her skill and competence. By herself she is assertive and forthright but she prefers to play second fiddle when Alan is around. She quietly asks Alan and me about what we know and how the accident happened. Her low-key demeanor is in contrast to her usual lively behavior and lends a serious, somber feeling.

Gwen tells me, "I'm sorry I didn't get here sooner. I just got it into my head that you were exaggerating."

"I don't blame you. I still can't believe what is happening." We hug and I say to everyone, "I'm really pleased that all you guys are here. I feel more at ease, since I know you will make sure that Phyllis gets the best help she can."

You are whisked into a spacious examination room and surrounded by an army in white.

"Lift your arms. Good, good—there is some function in the triceps. This will be a big help in the rehab phase."

"Press your fingers against mine. That's good. We have weak pressure in the thumb, index finger, and middle finger but nothing in the ring and pinky. Looks like damage in the C-six, C-seven level." Pinpricks are made and sensations or lack of them recorded.

I notice a chart on the wall showing the outline of the spinal cord and the nerves leading to the various external parts of the body. The chart reminds me of all the times I studied anatomy, but that was more than fifteen years ago. They are concentrating on your arms and fingers with their pinprick sensations. I am pleased to see that I can follow their explorations. Your thumb, index finger, and middle finger are responding to the pain caused by these pinpricks, letting the doctors know that the nerves reaching these areas are not damaged. Your ring and pinky fingers are barely sensitive, telling the doctors that these nerves are on the edge of the damage. When they try your forearm the same pattern is discernible. The nerves on the thumb side are working while the nerves on the pinky side are iffy. You have no sensations on the underside of your upper arm. In looking at the chart I can see how those nerves connect into the spinal cord. The pattern is clearly emerging that the damage is at the last two neck vertebrae and the first vertebra in the shoulder area. It all fits in with the information we have been given from the CAT scan.

I was taught in my biology study in college that nerves do not regenerate. My poor dear, I hope they have learned some new things since I went to school.

As the exam continues, I feel relieved. I know we have our best chance here for whatever help is possible.

Forty-five minutes later, the head orthopedic surgeon gives the team's assessment. "The seventh cervical vertebra and the first thoracic vertebra are dislocated. Your wife's spinal cord is bruised and in shock.

"The massive swelling is like the swelling caused by any bruise. Blood vessels have been broken and blood has been released into the injured area along with other fluids. In spinal cord injury, unlike a black eye, for instance, these fluids cause the death of nerves by cutting off oxygen to sensitive cells. It can take up to two years for the spinal cord to adjust to the traumatic changes. Unfortunately, the probability of nerve cells regrowing is remote. Unlike bones, which get broken and with time repair themselves, nerve cells don't. But we won't know for at least two years exactly what Mrs. York's abilities will be."

It is six o'clock in the evening when they take you to the operating room. It is important to reset your vertebrae as soon as possible.

Seeing you wheeled away by strangers leaves me feeling empty and powerless. I hate the thought of others caring for you because I am unable to.

When I was five years old my family disintegrated under the pressure of the Great Depression. My father had been out of work for several years and his father had grown tired of supporting us. We had been moving into seedier and seedier apartments in New York City, until finally there was no place left to go to. My father then abandoned us and my mother couldn't keep the family together. The New York City courts got involved and my older brother, my sister, and I were sent to a home/school named Leake and Watts in Yonkers, New York. I don't know whether the sign on the front lawn of this huge, old, one-time estate proclaimed Leake and Watts to be an orphanage, but for the approximately two hundred or so kids who lived there it was always called "the orphanage." I had been left to the care of strangers and now I am doing that to you. I hope these strangers do as well with you as my strangers did with me.

PHYLLIS

✳ You did well, beloved. I'm being put in traction to reset my vertebrae. The faces around me are wonderful. If I am going to make it, they will help me. I can relax. I'm glad, beloved, that you have friends with you now.

Oh, God, lots of Valium is wonderful. In my stupor, Freud comes to see me. He comments, "You had your accident on the twentieth anniversary of your mother's death. Doesn't that interest you?"

"Not at all," I scream. "It's just a coincidence. October is a bad month for our family."

Freud said, "Perhaps you defend yourself too quickly. Perhaps you do not want to know?"

"I was always a good daughter," I lie, knowing I abandoned my mother when she was close to death.

"My dear Phyllis, no one is always good to their mamma," he replies.

"How dare you accuse me of being a bad daughter. You, the dirty old man who created the term 'penis envy.' You must have become jealous of other men and now you have the nerve to say 'penis envy' is a female disease. How can I believe anything you say?"

"So," he says, "perhaps you are angry with me for showing you something you don't want to see. And you accuse me of being a dirty old man. You punish me the way you have punished yourself for being bad to your mamma."

DAVID

✳ How quickly my prayers have changed. At first I hoped

to see movement in your legs and now I fear to see you lose a little twitch in a finger.

Alan, Gwen, Teresa, her husband Tom, Heidi, and I settle into the major task of a patient's friends and relatives . . . waiting.

An hour later a doctor stops by to tell us, "We have put Mrs. York in traction. We've started with forty pounds but her neck muscles are very tight. We're giving her muscle relaxants, but it's going to be a long night."

In this high-anxiety situation we take the cure, we go to eat. It's hard to describe the feelings I am having. I am walking under water. Pushing hard to move and seeing people and events in a blurry, dream-like sequence. I resent the street people. The bums, the drunks walking around or sleeping on vents while you are threatened with the loss of being able to move your hands. I resent the couples sitting together as we so often had done. I resent how unfair life is.

My thoughts keep drifting back to the time when my brother and sister and I arrived at Leake and Watts just before the end of the summer of 1934. The other kids were away at camp so the place had an eerie, abandoned look. There was a huge, gray castle-like main house where the boys lived and where all the kids attended school. The girls lived in cottages scattered around the extensive grounds. The silence seemed ominous and I felt lost, wandering around in empty space. My strongest recollection of this Leake and Watts period is the fear I felt looking at illustrations in a book about the Wizard of Oz.

How can this be me here? How can you be in an operating room hoping to have three fingers working rather than two?

By the time we return from the restaurant it is nine thirty. Tom, Teresa, and Heidi go home. Alan, Gwen, and I return to our waiting. We watch people move in and out of the intensive care unit.

"Do you think the Phillies will win the playoffs?"

A doctor appears from time to time. "We're up to a hundred pounds but still no resetting."

"Are your kids Scott, Stephen, and Stacy going to be home for Thanksgiving, Gwen?"

Alan says, "David, I'll try Ilene again."

"We're up to a hundred and twenty pounds, still no change."

"I finally got Ilene. She said she'll be here tomorrow."

"How did she take it?"

"She cried. She has a girl friend with her. She's taking the train in the morning."

"I'm glad someone's with her."

"We're up to a hundred and forty pounds. No motion yet. We'll try ten more pounds and then we have to stop. If this doesn't work we will have to operate and set the vertebrae manually. We don't like to do this because it's riskier in terms of nerve damage."

"How's the shark-fishing?"

"Where is Scott applying to medical school?"

Finally, all our irrelevancies exhausted, we sit silent.

Suddenly, I jump up and shout, "Goddamn it!" and start pounding the wall with my fists.

Alan puts his arm around me, "David, you need your hands. You can't make a mess out of yourself, too."

"I know. I know. I'm just so goddamn angry." Alan hugs me, while Gwen cries.

A smiling doctor reports, "We're in luck. Phyllis's dislocation slipped back in place. She'll be coming up soon."

It is midnight. Twenty hours after the accident. You look exhausted but pleased with the success of your first small step. I catch your hand and squeeze it. Your answering squeeze is the barest of movements. Your right hand seems better but your left is worse. God! Couldn't we even get a small break? A finger, a little more movement? It isn't a lot to ask.

I cry as you enter the intensive care unit. Mourning my loss of you and the losses you are suffering.

---

* IV *

DAVID

✳   The thought of visiting you in intensive care is agonizing. I need to be there at eleven o'clock, even though visiting hours start at two. Ilene's train is due in at ten-thirty and I don't want her waiting alone to see you.

Ilene, our eldest daughter, is an attractive brunette who is more sophisticated than her sisters. She worked for Toughlove until a year ago when she decided that she wanted to go to graduate school and get a degree in tourism administration. Ilene comes by her interest in travel legitimately. In her young life she was subjected to our vagabond-like wanderings. Ilene was born in the Bronx, New York City. When she was seven we traded in the people-intensive city life for the rural quiet of Vermont. Six years later we migrated to San Diego, a small city whose pride and joy is its great weather, which we thought we would relish after the rigors of Vermont. But within a year we had packed up to try our hand in St. Croix in the U. S. Virgin Islands. The pleasures of our tropical sojourn waned quickly and a year and a half later we landed in suburban Pennsylvania. By now Ilene was a full-fledged travel bug and in high school she became an exchange student living with a family in West

Germany. She chose a college that allowed her to spend semesters living in different countries and used the opportunities to live in Colombia and in Mérida, Mexico.

She has moved to Washington, D. C., and is attending George Washington University. Ilene is excited about her courses and loves living in metropolitan Washington rather than in our rural environment.

In the intensive care waiting room two other anguished families sit and wait. They huddle together to absorb what little comfort they can from each other. They speak in the hushed tones frequently heard at funerals. Sitting by myself, I feel lonely and excluded. I keep looking down the hall waiting for Ilene to appear. Finally, I recognize her trim figure, suitcase in hand, as she looks tentatively around.

"Ilene, Ilene, over here," I call out. We both hurry toward each other and hug, letting our tears fall. I take her suitcase and we walk toward the waiting room, talking.

"How are you, Dad?"

"I'm okay. Tired, I guess. We didn't leave here until after twelve last night. I spent the night at Alan and Gwen's house. I couldn't stand the thought of going home."

"Do you have any information on Mom? I only got a little from Alan last night."

I recite yesterday's events and fill Ilene in on what I know so far. Ilene has always been a stickler for details, so it takes us a while. Talking allows us both to relax and adjust to our new roles as relatives of the badly injured.

"Ilene, how come you brought a suitcase?"

"I want to stay here with you, Dad. I can't concentrate on my schoolwork and I have to be here with Mom. Is it okay?"

"Ilene, my dearest, you are such a comfort; it's more than okay. I want you to stay." Again, we tearfully collapse into each other's arms.

"Dad, what happened to your hands, your knuckles are all bruised?"

"Yeah, I know. Last night I got stupid and started hitting the wall. Luckily I didn't break anything."

A nurse appears and tells us that we can visit the patients in the intensive care unit, only she calls it "the ICU," which takes me a minute to translate. We move toward the two huge swinging doors. I have noticed that people push something on the side of the doors to open them.

I push the large metal plate on the side of the wall and the huge swinging doors ease open, inviting Ilene and me into an Hieronymus Bosch landscape. On each side are cubicles containing once-human forms that are now in various degrees of mummification. Beds are being rotated, twisting and turning in seemingly random motion while passive occupants are like astronauts floating in space attached to respirators that hiss up and down giving breath to the breathless; fluids drip into the almost lifeless and quiet agony permeates the hall. I escape into your room only to find that you who were always so alive are now a fragile thing that needs constant tending. The loss of your chest muscles leaves you breathless if you talk. The traction on your neck and the immobility of your body make you seem like a head suspended, an impression that the small movements of your hands and arms only exaggerate. When I hold your hand you say it feels as if it is on fire. Your body sensations alternate between pins and needles and fire.

I ask one of the omnipresent nurses if your feelings of fire and pins and needles are unusual in spinal cord injury.

"No, the injury makes the spinal fluid acidic which causes the burning sensation. We are giving Mrs. York some medication which will help relieve these symptoms. The pins and needles are from the damaged nerves and they will soon go away."

You try to pay attention to Ilene and me but it is obvious that you can't respond to us, so we sit there quietly mourning.

A nurse tells us that our daughter, Jodi, is outside with her baby. Jodi would like one of us to watch the baby so she can visit. I volunteer, knowing it will give me some respite from the ICU agony.

Jodi and I embrace. "I'm glad you came, my dear. I know Mom wants to see you even if she can't really pay much attention to anything right now."

"I'm sorry to bring Nitya, but I couldn't get a baby-sitter and I couldn't stay away any longer."

"Don't worry. I'll watch her. You go on inside. I'll have one of the nurses get you if Nitya needs you."

Jodi has brought Nitya's stroller and the baby is sitting in it watching the activity of the hospital. I take her on a trip through the halls and follow the ins and outs of the passageways. Jefferson Hospital is built around a central atrium. Here, on the ninth floor, the hallways keep going around, creating a big circle. This circle allows Nitya and me to take a long walk. We stop at other waiting rooms along the way and explore the intricate layout of the hospital. I enjoy the relief that our trip allows. Forty-five minutes later I return to the ICU to find Ilene and Jodi sitting outside.

"Dad, where were you? Visiting hours are over until tonight. We thought you got lost."

"No, I just took Nitya on a tour of the hospital. Was Mom all right when you left?"

"Yeah, she's really out of it though. What's going to happen?"

"I don't know. We just have to wait and see. If Mom is stabilized, they will bring her outside the ICU tomorrow until they can operate. The doctor said that they've scheduled Mom in two more days if she is physically able. They will take a piece of bone from her hip and place it next to her unstable neck and shoulder vertebrae and wire it in place so the vertebrae can't move and fray more of her spinal nerves."

Jodi needs to go home now. She has a two-hour drive ahead of her and the next visiting hours aren't until six tonight. Ilene and I walk Jodi and Nitya to their car and watch them drive away. Slowly we walk to a restaurant to get something to eat. We fill the time talking about school and work and anything but what has brought us here.

After supper we take our posts at the ICU and finish our mostly silent vigil. At the end of visiting hours a nurse informs us that you will be transferred to the step-down unit tomorrow. This means you will be in a room just down the hall. It also means that you are out of the most critical phase for now.

Ilene and I drive to Alan and Gwen's. We have both agreed that we would rather stay there than at our house.

PHYLLIS

✳   I'm on a rotisserie. Flipped this way and that. All my

friends lie on the floor and talk to me when I am upside down. Did you know that drinking milkshakes upside down makes you vomit? Beloved, you look so worried.

I'm sorry that I have ruined our life.

I keep asking everyone not to abandon me as my father did, so long ago.

DAVID

✳ Hooray! You made it out of intensive care for a few days. They are waiting to operate to fuse your unstable vertebrae. A change from machinery, tubes, and desperate feelings, but they have created a new torture for you. It is called a Stryker Frame. A bed on which you are rotated like an animal on a spit.

Your head is held rigid by forty pounds of traction and they cover you with another frame to roll you over on your stomach.

You need to be off your back and on your stomach for ten minutes every hour to prevent bedsores, a potential problem created by your inability to move your body and keep the blood circulating. By rotating you every so often they hope to ward off an evil to which you are now vulnerable. Little by little we are learning about the wonders of creation. These are biology lessons I do not want.

In the face-downward position there is an opening for your face. I lie on the floor to talk to you. Much of our conversation is a monologue by me, quite a switch from our usual style.

Lying on your stomach on this torture rack is like everything else about this damned injury—necessary, difficult, and painful.

On the way home from the hospital I share my thoughts and feelings with Ilene.

"I can't stand the idea of going to our house. The memories of what was are too painful for what is." Ilene pats my shoulder and says, "I know." I look over and see a large tear drip down her lovely face.

I change the subject. "Ilene, you know we've been having a battle with our business manager. He wants us to stop the free referral service we've been doing. He says it's bankrupting us. Mom and I insist that unless we supply this service Toughlove will never grow. We've talked to him about finding some additional ways to support Toughlove. I guess this accident was the last straw for him. He submitted his letter of resignation today. On top of this, our lease is up and the landlord wants to raise our rent. To tell the truth, I don't have the time, energy, or interest for any of it. I can't even think about it.

"Dad, I have an idea. Why don't you move Teresa and Gwen into your house and have Toughlove work out of there? It will put the business right at hand and help you save on rent."

"That sounds good. I think I'll call them tomorrow and set it up. Thanks, Ilene." I reach over and pat her hand.

To myself I think, "I wonder what Phyllis would have said." God, how I miss her.

───── ⁂ V ⁑ ─────

PHYLLIS

⁂ They are trying to kill me here. They are giving me two pints of blood to cure my anemia before they operate tomorrow. I'll probably get AIDS. Let me die by my own failings, not someone else's. Please.

DAVID

⁂ It's been four days since your accident and this morning they roll you out for another trip to the operating room. You will have some bone removed from your hip to fuse your vertebrae. After that you will be put in a neck brace called a halo. A metal frame is screwed into your skull and supported in place by metal struts attached to a large pad resting on your shoulders and chest.

You will need sweat clothes with zippers in front to fit over the bulky contraption surrounding your head and shoulders.

Heidi, Ilene, Jodi, Nitya, and I have come to share the vigil. We have been warmed with the usual hospital comforts: "Phyllis's mobility may increase, decrease, or stay the same." We share the sitting room and our anxieties with a couple whose son has just entered intensive care and a woman whose husband has been here for several months. We huddle together in the camaraderie of waiting. Nitya entertains us or sleeps quietly in her stroller. We are all grateful for the distraction.

Heidi tells us, "I wake up every morning now, realizing that my life will never be the same. I know I have to take charge of my marriage and my kids. I know that I'm the only one in my marriage that is going to make changes. I'm looking for a place to live and I have to start getting a divorce. I can't stand my life right now." We all hug Heidi and tell her how pleased we are with her decision.

The reality of what Heidi has said—that life would never be the same—is painful. Each of us in our own way is struggling to come to terms with the sudden recognition of how tentative our own lives are. The sharing of our grief and fear is more binding than all the other struggles our family has gone through.

After four hours the doctor finally comes to speak with us. The operation has gone well, but he has no idea about changes in movement. They wheel you by and we talk for a minute. The horrible metal halo surrounding your head looks painful. At least the Stryker Frame is gone. I'm not sure it's a fair trade.

"How are you, sweetheart?" I say.

"Okay."

"I love you."

"I love you."

"Can you move your fingers?" Your right hand is more active but your left hand is limp.

You ask, "Is it okay?"

"Yes, dear," I lie. We never get good news without a dose of bad.

PHYLLIS

✳ It seems this room is always dark. And I'm never alone.

The doctor tells me some of my fingers will work, my hand and arms will function, but below my armpits—nothing . . . and no bladder or bowel control, no feelings, and no orgasm.

But I know that the only half-normal feelings I'm having right now are between my legs. Even though I'm embarrassed, I tell the nurse, who says, "You never know what can happen with spinal cord injury. If you have feeling anywhere, that's a great place to have it."

How do I keep my dignity when my anal sphincter doesn't move to a strange doctor's touch? But if he touches my clitoris my anus works. Oh, my God, not only don't I know my ass from my elbow, but now I don't know my clitoris from my behind. Find a girl friend, fast, beloved.

My blood pressure is plummeting. I seem to be a head without a body. The nurses are running around like crazy. Look, beloved, I'm dying. It doesn't hurt at all. It doesn't matter. It's just a fact. Let me go.

They tell me, "It's nothing serious. Your body can't adjust to your blood pressure like it used to. It will get better."

DAVID

❋ After two days you have made it out of intensive care for good and London, England, has called. They want us to be on a TV show.

It brought back memories of the good time we had when Thames Television came to film us walking through Central Park in New York City and talking about our work with Toughlove parents and kids.

I know it's important for our business, but how can I leave you now? How can I talk to you about my going when I know how much you would have loved to make the trip? I can't stand the thought of your being hurt more than you are. Yet, I know that I want to go and that I will go. I feel guilty even to think it, but I'm looking forward to escaping the pressure cooker of your accident.

I finally get to call Teresa about Toughlove. "I'm okay. Phyllis is holding her own," I say, even though time has lost its meaning. "I was talking to Ilene about Art's quitting and the landlord raising the rent, funding the referral system, and everything we're going through, when smart, practical Ilene came up with what may be a solution. She suggested we move the office and you and Gwen into our house. That way we save rent and it gives us time to see what we're doing."

"That's a great idea, David. See how you never know who can give you something good. There will be some problems, though. We are going to have to change our mailing address and our phone number. Cash flow will suffer for a while. I think the only way we can do it is by reducing the salaries that Gwen and I make. By scrimping and saving I'm sure we'll pull through."

"How can I ask you guys to make less money when you make so little now? Phyllis and I don't take any salary but we can cut back on the royalties we are getting from the books we sell. Maybe that will give us enough."

"No, David, you and Phyllis have been carrying Toughlove for years now. I think we'll do whatever has to be done."

"Thank you, Teresa. I'll have to go to the house and move things around even though I can't stand the thought of going there.

"Teresa, I don't know what to do about England. I would like to go, but I don't feel I can leave Phyllis now that she has that God-awful halo on her head."

"I know how hard it is to make these choices"—and I know that Teresa really does know—"but Phyllis is out of intensive care, she's stabilized, and we are here with her. Go, it will be good for Toughlove. I'll call and confirm your reservation. Phyllis will understand."

"No she won't," and we both laugh. "I really dread telling Phyllis."

Teresa in her most soothing voice coos, "I know."

PHYLLIS

❋   My new room is filled to overflowing with flowers, plants, and friends. I'm suffocating.

I'm in a brace called a halo. I can't move. It's the kind of halo only a Jewish saint would have.

I'm choking to death. I wish I hadn't come into the hospital with a cold. The nurse pushes on my diaphragm and every two hours they put a pipe down my throat to remove the phlegm I can't cough up anymore. Taking my next breath between the suctioning and the pushing is about all I can manage. I think I'd rather die.

DAVID

✳ Alan and Gwen come to visit at night. Alan celebrates your release from intensive care in our usual way. He sits by your bedside, "Phyllis, have a shrimp. Take a bite. You like shrimp. These are extra large. You'll like them."

"Alan, I can't," you whisper.

"C'mon Phyllis, these are really good shrimp. We got them at the fish store you like," coaxes Gwen.

They know how the magic of food has been able to raise you from the dead. It always made you feel better. Tonight, suctioning and breathing seem all you can manage. I can't add my going to London to your burdens now.

PHYLLIS

✳ Who the hell am I, anyway? Please tell me. I have all kinds of new and important decisions to make. Would I rather lie on my right side for two hours or my left side for two hours? Would I rather go to the bathroom sitting up or lying down?

How would I like it if only my left hand worked and not my right? People keep saying it's better to have your arms than your legs.

Today a friend of a friend came whom I barely knew. She became angry with me for my pain, my grief, my self-pity, and my loss. She had her own grief, which I can only imagine. She obviously hated to feel it, or otherwise why was she being so mean to me? She kept asking me to decide which was worse—to have a dead son or a spinal cord injury? As if there is a choice. Pain is pain.

But there is something that I do know. God is no woman. A woman would have never given me this injury and my period, too.

DAVID

✳ Now I have to tell Phyllis that I'm leaving for London tomorrow.

"What is it, David?" you whisper.

"Do you remember that I told you about London wanting us for a TV show? Well, I told them I'm coming. They've arranged for me to fly out tomorrow and I agreed."

"David," Phyllis says with the tears streaming down her face, "how can you leave me? I'm so scared when you're not here."

"I know, Phyllis. I feel awful leaving you now, but I have to go. I've arranged to fly over tomorrow, do the show the next day, and return the day after."

Between your tears you say, "I'm sorry, dearest. I know you have to go. You're my security blanket and I feel so frightened all the time now. Please be careful and come back to me."

"Don't worry. I won't get hurt and I'll be back in three days."

"David, you'll be so tired. Why don't you stay a few more days. I'll be all right."

"No, Phyllis, I want to be here as much as I can. While I'm gone, dearest, sleep cradled in my love."

Your tears stop and you smile and say, "I will, my love."

Parting is really hard tonight.

PHYLLIS

✳ The nurse tells me, "We're moving you to the rehab floor tomorrow. You're not ill, just injured."

"But I feel sick."

"You're not, it's just your body reacting to the injury."

Will I always feel like this?

───── ✳ VI ✳ ─────

DAVID

✳ I pack my clothes along with my guilt and fly off to London. As usual I retreat into intellectualizing about other people's problems to avoid the reality of my own. I am curious to see if the problems parents are having with teenagers in England are the same as those in America.

I push my thoughts and feelings about you away and concentrate on presenting our Toughlove program. It is a relief to act as if everything is all right. Outside the storm roars and dances. Inside is an eerie silence. I know we have passed through the medically critical period of life—or death. We now face the pain of learning to make a life with what remains. The respite and adventure of London is a hollow reminder of what our life had been. I miss that life and what you were. But I've got to put these maudlin, self-pitying thoughts away. You and I will need all the strength and hope we can muster.

PHYLLIS

✳ I have been moved to the third floor where the rehab is located. The room where they put me is ugly, dim, with walls the greenish gray color of ice plants on cemetery graves. It is crowded with three yellow old ladies with casts or missing legs and me. The clean, crisp, blue whiteness of the room upstairs is gone and so are you, my dearest, off to London.

Do you know that there is a night supervisor of nurses who watches over me like a guardian angel? Kay, my ICU nurse, comes to visit. And you, beloved, are in London being famous. What do you care?

Tonight Jodi is holding a healing session over me. Eight sisters from the ashram are "Omming" me right out of the bed. My roommates sleep through it all.

"Ma, think positive, it will help."

"Jodi, I know that if you could you would pray me whole."

"Yes, I would. I will pray for you. Ma, please visualize your spinal cord healing. You have to believe. I'll leave my guru's affirmation tape for you to hear. It's very relaxing."

When they leave, all the sisters wish me well and God's love. Jodi leans over the bed with Nitya in her arms.

"Goodnight, dear baby." How I want to touch her.

"I'll see you tomorrow, Ma. I'll put on the tape, okay?"

"Sure." As Jodi leaves I hear the soothing, calm Indian voice of Jodi's guru assuring me that God loves me.

I sleep protected in the warmth of Gurieji's voice and Jodi's love.

DAVID

✳ London is lonely without you. The TV show staff is very courteous and attentive but I feel as if I'm only going through the motions of being here. In spite of my feelings I force myself to be lively for the cameras. Everyone I meet responds enthusiastically so I assume I came over okay.

My head is back home with you and I calculate the time and send you a telegram: "My dearest, I love you. I can't wait to be next to you."

The next day I'm flying back. It's as though I'd never gone to London at all.

❋ Tonight, David's loving telegram, which is hung on my bulletin board along with my family's pictures, does not soothe me. I have had hiccups and nausea for hours and there is a doctor on duty tonight who gives everyone laxatives, enemas, and other pains in the ass. God, help me.

Hooray for me. No matter how hard Doctor Anal tried, he couldn't find a bowel impaction. He gives me an injection of calming Compazine so I can sleep.

In the morning it looks as if every member of our thousand Toughlove support groups has sent a card. The mail comes in by the bag-load. It makes me cry and cry. Every verse in every other card is signed by Helen Rice Steiner. Who is she, anyway?

Jefferson Hospital is doing research on preventing blood clots as a result of spinal injury operations. I am one of their guinea pigs.

Did you know that doctors get mad at you for failing their blood-clot studies?

I am now on blood thinner and Toughlove has hit London and you are a smash on TV. Maybe you don't need me anymore.

I have a bedsore. The nurses are upset. They wash it with peroxide and saline. They bandage and unbandage it. "It doesn't look good." "It's not too terrible." "We have to watch it." "Are you doing your weight shifts?" "Make sure you lie on your side, not your back." "Don't stay in one place too long."

"Your bedsore seems innocuous, but these little surface sores can expand underneath the skin until serious complications and even death can occur. They can plague people with your kind of injury."

The staff says, "It is not quite a decubitus, it is more like a kissing-type sore. Some people get those sores because of the shape of their backside. You are one of them."

Bessie, my roommate, lets me know how powerless I am.

This scrawny, eighty-six-year-old woman with a broken leg has become the bane of my existence. With her little knife she chops up prunes night and day, eats crackers in the middle of the night, and lives and breathes for the bedpan. Her radio and light click on and off all night long. She demands attention from anyone who walks into the room. She won't let me sleep.

"Nurse! Nurse! I think I have to go."

"Bessie, you just went."

"Yes, but this time I have to BM," Bessie whines.

"You BM-ed four times this morning! You've got to stop drinking prune juice and eating all those prunes."

"Please, give me the bedpan."

"Okay, okay," sighs the nurse, "but you better go."

Then, "Bessie, that's only one drop of urine."

"Well, I had to weewee." And on and on it goes until I'm insane.

When she is not BM-ing, weeweeing, or eating, Bessie is complaining.

"Doctor, Doctor, today the nurse wouldn't give me the bedpan. My bowels are not moving. The physical therapy is too much for me."

She reveals her pain by a series of short howls. Ooow! Ooow! Barking like a little Chihuahua dog at least six hundred times a day. Her seventy-two-year-old nephew is Bessie's only visitor.

The physical therapist comes to stretch my leg muscles and move my joints. The occupational therapist has given me a soft ball to open and close my fist around.

I want to brush my own teeth. No small task. The nurse places a toothbrush in my fist. I hold it the way my children held their first spoons, like a shovel. I move my arm back and forth.

The nurse waits with two cups. One cup with water and one cup empty. Each cup has a straw. I rinse my mouth with the water and spit it into the empty cup. The nurse opens the toothpaste and puts it on the toothbrush for me. I brush and brush just because I can do it. I know you will be glad for me and I am anxious to show you my skill.

DAVID

✳ I've been gone three days but much has happened. Your flowers have spilled over so that all your roommates, the nurses, and other patients are sharing in the deluge. I am touched and pleased.

You smile and cry as I lean over the bed to kiss your cheek. "Doesn't the halo hurt? I can't get used to seeing you in it. Is it all right if I hold your hand?"

"I want you to, David, but my hands still hurt me when they are touched. But, you know something, my teeth will rot out of my head. I've tried flossing but my hands just won't work."

"Well, we've paid Alan too much money to keep your mouth in shape and he'll kill us if we don't keep his reputation up. So, open up and let your in-house dental technician take charge."

You open wide as I adjust the light, measure a length of dental floss, and assume my professional caring role. It feels good to be doing something physical with you, even if it is only flossing teeth. "Well, Mrs. York, do you need novocaine?"

Your eyes are laughing and your muffled response around my hands in your mouth sounds appropriately dental. "Thanks for your compliments, my dear, but just keep your mouth open."

The everyday task is a relief from the heaviness of the hospital. The best part is your laughter.

Then comes the big event you have been saving up: brushing your own teeth. I begin the ritual preparation: a toothbrush with toothpaste, a cup full of water with a bendable straw. From there on it is all downhill. It is a juggling match between the toothbrush, the water for rinsing, and the empty cup for spitting into. The whole event is orchestrated by a straw that slips, falls, or bends the wrong way. We are both wet and frustrated. You start crying and say, "I want to die. What the hell good am I? I can't even brush my teeth." I feel I have let you down by not being quick or perceptive enough. I leave your bedside in tears for a lonely hour-long drive to Alan and Gwen's. Even Ilene's company and talk can't rouse me.

It's been four days that you have been on the rehab floor and now comes another milestone. They are starting to raise your bed so eventually you can sit up. Even a few inches and your energy level drops to zero. Without the use of the muscles to circulate blood from below your armpits, your blood pressure drops instantly. Everyone hopes that this will subside and that you'll be in a wheelchair next week. The thought of you being up and around seems too good to be true. But the thought of you in a wheelchair is chilling.

On the way to Alan and Gwen's Ilene tells me, "Dad, I think it's time for me to go back to Washington. Is it okay with you? I want to stay but. . . ."

"Yeah, Ilene. I know you have to go. We'll be okay. Mom is beginning to get better and you need to get on with your life. I'm glad you came. I don't know how I would have managed without you. Anyway, I've got to go back to our house and begin preparations for the Toughlove office moving into it."

The next day Ilene and I stop at the hospital so she can say good-bye.

"Ma, I'm going back to Washington tonight. I hate to leave you. Is it all right?"

"Yes, my dear, of course. I love you. I'll miss you."

Ilene picks up her suitcase and starts for the door with tears flowing down her face. I am moving toward her when a nurse's aide enters the room and, seeing Ilene, puts her arm around her.

"Phyllis will be all right. We'll take good care of her. I think she is very special. But, now it's time to stop crying. This is life. You mustn't cry in front of your mother."

She walks her out to the elevator. I miss Ilene already. The nurse's aide has won a spot in my heart.

✳ VII ✳

PHYLLIS

✳ Five people come to lift me out of bed into a wheelchair. Because of my blood pressure, I have to lie down in the wheelchair too.

When I try to sit up, even a little, darkness settles in as I start to faint. My new mobility means I can go to the dining room.

I feel like Olivia De Havilland in *The Snake Pit*. I see a disjointed, surreal world through the shadow of my halo. The people in the dining room are all in some state of disarray, disease, and demise. At my table Mary dribbles cheese-filled spittle as the nurse feeds her. The legless lady never looks up from her plate, and the man who had a stroke smiles because he can't talk. The TV set blares away.

IVs hang out of people while their electronic monitors ring and ping. I am being wheeled down the hall lying in my wheelchair, halo brace to my waist. I see myself in the mirror and cry.

You should see what I look like. My breasts fall out to each side and sit in my sweat jacket pockets like basketballs.

Now they've told me I have to socialize with other patients. Save me!

DAVID

✳ Like everything else, the wheelchair is a mixed blessing. You can't sit up straight yet and the halo weighs you down like an anchor. Every half-hour you must be "weight-shifted." It means you have to be tilted backward into a lying position. This will prevent the pooling of blood below your buttocks due to the pressure of sitting. We have to put you in different positions to prevent more skin breakdown from the pooling. The simple mechanisms of your body no longer work. There is so much to learn and do.

We get to eat in the dining room now, another dubious pleasure. Patients and their families are scattered around the room. Some of the employees have the TV going while they eat. Wheelchairs move in and out pulling movable stands holding various intravenously fed fluids. The liquids are monitored by machines that keep a constant beeping going. Occasionally one of the machines lets out a low wail. Nurses and orderlies converge on the errant device and failing patient. On top of all this you have become supersensitive to noise and movement. We have been told you are suffering from sensory overload. Another benefit of your injury.

Your meal routine consists of finding a time when the dining room is relatively empty, moving to an isolated table, and getting ready to eat. First you need to be weight-shifted. I put the brakes on your chair and lean you backward onto my lap. Ten minutes later you sit up. We contact the person delivering the food and find your tray. By the time the food arrives you need to be weight-shifted again. Next we move you up to the table but your semiupright position prevents you from seeing your food. Eventually we get the logistics solved and you begin to eat. The TV and beepers warm up. Sensory overload begins and we rush out to the safety of your room.

Soon it's time for you to go back to bed. Five sturdy people enter. Bessie, your roommate, waylays each one with a request or a complaint. Finally, Bessie is tended to and an episode out of a Mack Sennett movie occurs. The five sturdy people climb up and down your bed, pushing, pulling, lifting, sometimes working together, sometimes at cross-purposes. After awhile, you are lying on the bed exhausted. Five less sturdy-looking people exit.

I watch in awe and leave the hospital panicked. How the hell am I ever going to manage all this?

PHYLLIS

✳ My visitors irk Bessie. She asks me, "How come you have so much company?" I answer, "Because I'm nice and people like me."

"My friends," she tells me, "are too old to visit. My family is either dead or they live too far away." I feel a pang of compassion for her, but in another moment she manages to alienate me further. "You get so much attention from the nurses, how come?"

"Bessie, it's because I can't do anything for myself, except brush my teeth badly. I'm paralyzed. It takes two nurses and three helpers to get me out of bed and I'm just learning to sit up straight in the wheelchair. I'm paralyzed, Bessie, that's why." Bessie replies with deep snores. I feel ashamed of myself for wanting to kill her. I yell out, "Drop dead, Bessie," and Bessie snores on.

I lie in bed and try to project myself across the room, making sure the points of my halo land in her eyes and kill her. Thank God for Ellen, my other roommate. She has had a stroke and is older and sicker than Bessie, but she is wonderful. She loves art and is polite. I feel very protective of her. I hope Ellen gets better. As for Bessie, God forgive me, I hope she breaks the other leg and goes to another hospital.

My guilt brings back the memory of the summer when my mother told me, "Grandpa had a stroke. He'll live with Aunty and we will help him."

By ten o'clock every summer morning my grandfather and I are sitting on our folding chairs in front of his apartment building. We are reading the newspapers I stopped to buy on the way to his house. We read aloud to each other. We have lunch together and sometimes go to the movies. We miss my grandmother who died a few months ago. We share our memories of her: Friday nights when she gave out presents for all of us; how she called Grandpa by his last name "Scharf" except when she was angry and then she used both his names, "Ben Scharf." He teaches me about numbers and to count change. HIs old-man friends come and talk with him in the afternoon while I play pitching pennies, baseball cards, dolls—with kids that live around there. At five or six I take him upstairs where my aunt waits with his supper. I walk the few blocks alone to my house, being careful not to step on a crack in the sidewalk so I won't break my mother's back. But when I want it to rain, I step on ants.

In September, after my ninth birthday I leave my grandfather and go back to school. One day soon after that, my father meets me when I get home from school.

"Grandpa has died." I'm not surprised. I feel hurt and cry.

My blood pressure is adapting. Five people are no longer needed to schlep me out of bed into the wheelchair. They now stand-pivot me. One person can do it, but they have another for backup just in case. The halo and I are not easy to move. Here's how it's done. The bed's wound up. My legs are put over the side and pulled toward the floor. The nurse holds my knees tightly between her legs, her arms around my back. I reach up and hang on to her. She lifts me, pivots toward the wheelchair, and plops me in.

If she misses or I miss, she lowers me to the floor, trying to make sure my jellyfish body isn't crumpled beneath me. When this happens, four other hysterical people appear and they put me back to bed. The doctor arrives with a crystal ball to make sure I didn't break anything. Once this is done, we start over.

In occupational therapy, I'm practicing pulling up a zipper—which I can do, buttoning buttons—which I struggle to do, and lacing shoes and tying a bow—which I can't do.

"Later you'll type to strengthen your fingers," the therapist assures me.

"I couldn't type before, how will I do it now?"

He laughs and says, "You'll practice."

I am learning to weight-shift every half-hour. The staff people remind me to watch the clock and ask to be shifted. The arm of my wheelchair is taken off, I'm tilted sideways onto a person's lap. This is on the closest I get to anyone. Intimacy is now down to relieving the pressure on my ass.

I can't wait to lie in your arms, dear.

I am able to take part in physical therapy now.

The PT room seems chaotic, but it isn't. It is crowded with orange and blue mats on short wooden legs. Everyone struggles to move, some do better than others. Each mat holds two of us. Legless, quads, paras, stroke victims, young, old, black, and white lie next to each other. We are all equal—pain, grief, and loss are our common denominator.

The physical therapist shows me my routine: twenty arm lifts on the pulleys to strengthen my upper arms. Since I have no grip, my hands are covered with mittens and Velcroed to the pulley. I can't stand being more confined.

Back on the mat, twenty-pound weights are put on my stomach just below my ribs, to strengthen my diaphragm in order to help me breathe. The muscles connecting my ribs aren't working anymore. Damn! Soon I'll have to learn to propel my own wheelchair.

Physical therapy makes for strange bedfellows. Next to me, fighting his therapist all the way, is a young man who keeps yelling to a friend on another mat, "Yo, Chuckie." Chuckie responds with a "Yo, Sal." Every five minutes or so this abortive South Philadelphia conversation goes on. To me, lying between them, they say nothing. Thank God for small favors.

I suspect that Sal probably stole my radio. I spend time finding out about him from the staff. Sal, they tell me, broke into a Y at night and jumped into an empty swimming pool. He broke his neck. He still sells dope but now it's from an electric wheelchair. His folks won't take him home. "He's just too mean," they told the staff.

The hair on my face grows faster than the hair on my legs. I am so vain I can't stand knowing it's there. I feel like I'm the bearded lady. Heidi tweezes my face.

"Heidi, I feel like the old schizophrenic women I saw when I worked at a mental health clinic. They all had long white hairs on their chins. I think I look like them."

"C'mon Ma."

"What if I can never tweeze my face?"

"I'll come every few days and tweeze or wax your face, as needed. Don't worry."

"Thank you. This is so embarrassing."

You, my dearest, you even floss my teeth. I can't believe how caring you are. Even though I've had the worst luck in this accident, I have the best in you guys. I'm sure if I asked, you would say, "I'll dental floss your teeth forever, if you can't. It's the kind of obsessive task I like." In my mind I answer you both with, "Soon you will feel burdened and tired of me." I don't think life with hair on my face and gum trouble is worth living.

Today I sit at the doors of the physical therapy room and witness a chamber of horrors where deformed, molested bodies try to make a crippled comeback. It is another of my versions of hell except there are no burn victims here. Limbless people struggle to walk, or "ambulate," as they say in this world. Artificial limbs, crutches, electric wheelchairs, casts, and braces offend my eyes. I am jealous of the patients who can walk, especially the really old people who leave their wheelchairs to struggle on their own two feet supported by two handrails. "Hey! I'm younger. Let me walk."

I see a quad in a halo just like me. He is lying on a mat trying to exercise his legs. He struggles, sweats, pushes, pulls, and turns red. I watch, awed at his courage. I could never be that brave. I cry and cry, thinking of his bravery. I'll call him Prince Valiant.

I watch Prince Valiant and his wife/helper, Aleta, in the dining room. He cannot use his arms and hands and she feeds him. She is here all the time. Where are you, beloved? How come you are less dedicated? His princess comes early and stays until night.

I ask the nurse about him. Prince Valiant dove into a swimming pool and broke his neck. He is a computer analyst. His legs may work but his hands may not.

I cannot believe how cruel life is.

Everyone comes to visit all the time. I don't get to talk to anyone, not even you. I am irritable. I want you alone, as I always have. Getting space for our love was always difficult. Your school, career, three children growing up. There has been space in the last few years and our love has been good. Now I don't feel that you're there. I feel you must be very angry with me for causing you so much pain.

"David, are you very angry with me?"

"Of course not, my dearest, how could I be?"

My chubby doctor tells me that quads don't need many calories. "If they go home and eat like they used to, they get fat." Ugh!

God is no woman, I tell myself once again. No woman would have given me this injured body, a fat problem, and my period too. Is there no redeeming piece to this tragedy? Well, right now I have no appetite. Eating takes too much energy. So for the second time in my fat life I'm being encouraged to eat. I can still remember the first time. It was after I had my tonsils out and my mother said to me, "Es, babula." I forgot to stop. Now even food does not comfort me. This time food cannot make things better.

"I feel like a broken doll," and you shake your head in agreement and I see your pain in the tears that fill your eyes. Today I feel like one of those Victorian dolls with the rag body and the big, heavy porcelain head.

Yesterday was worse. "Oh, David, the occupational therapist brought me a stick with a hook on the end to pull up my pants with. I was too weak to do it. I will never use it. I felt like a puppet. I cried and hid my face in shame."

"You're getting ahead of yourself, my dear. For now just do what you can."

The nurses tell me, "Wait until the halo's off; things will be better."

They want to comfort me. I won't allow myself to be comforted. If I need sticks and hooks for pants, will I never be able to see or reach my crotch again? The entire staff and all my friends have a better view of my vagina than I do. I am on display in a store window: a puppet, a dummy, a rag doll.

DAVID

❋ Finally you are sitting upright. You can weight-shift by

leaning sideways on my lap. "Phyllis, I love holding you even in this strained position, at least we can talk and be with each other." This small intimacy is a reminder of the pleasure we once had.

Now that you have achieved an upright position, physical therapy has begun. I'm shown how to "range" you. A process in which your ankles, knees, and hips have to be flexed and straightened; otherwise they will fuse and become unmovable. You squeeze a soft foam-rubber ball with your hands to increase strength and, we hope, movement.

You exhale into a clear plastic device. It has three cylinders with a blue ball in each cylinder. The harder you can blow, the higher the balls go. Without your chest muscles your diaphragm needs to be strengthened and this forced exhaling helps.

I learn how to help you cough or sneeze by sharply pushing upward just below your rib cage. Our needs are so basic, so primitive. Physical and occupational therapy provide my *first* real chance to talk to others. To see and hear how they are coping. A young, black man named Ike and his friend are there. I can quickly see the advantage he has with his upper body strength. He is able to move and manage himself pretty well. He was hurt in a football game. His friend is there to help and share gossip about others. Their warmth and camaraderie is contagious. An older white man fell off a ladder while painting his porch. He is a quiet country person who barely talks but works hard at his recovery. He has no visitors since he lives over two hundred miles away.

The kid Phyllis believes stole her radio rides around in his battery-powered wheelchair and gives the therapists a hard time.

The finale of PT is wheeling out of the room. You need to do as much as you can for yourself and you strain at the task. So far, you have managed five feet, but a small bump in the floor has you stymied. Another problem is steering. You unerringly head for a wall and get stuck. I feel my own muscles working to make your trip easier and I share your hurt and anger as tears of frustration and fury flow down your face.

We get to travel around a little now. I push you through the halls and we stop to weight-shift and talk in various waiting rooms. On nice days we look out of the glass-walled passageway over 11th Street. The view of the street with people hustling about framed by the city skyline is something you always enjoyed. We can't stay too long because you get cold. A new event for you. I was always the one to get cold while you complained of the heat.

── ✳ VIII ✳ ──

DAVID

✳ This morning I pack my things. I am moving out of Alan and Gwen's house and going back home. Alan and Gwen have invited me to stay as long as I like, but I know it is time for me to go.

I take all the back roads that we had become familiar with, but they look different somehow. The clusters of houses that had personalities and were occupied by people we recognized have become strange houses inhabited by strangers. The fields that once yielded the beauty of the changing seasons are only fields again. The nice old stone house on the corner of Tollgate Road, that has a sleigh filled with presents in front of it every Christmas, is distant and cold. The drive down the winding hill to where our house sits on a perilous bend makes me angry. I enter our house and turn my eyes away from the stairway that changed our life.

I want to burn the damned place down. I should be able to rig some kind of system that will make it look like faulty wiring caused it. We have stored lots of books and papers under the stairs—a perfect place for spontaneous combustion. My mind is racing through the possibilities until I begin to see the items we have collected, shared, and loved during our twenty-seven years of marriage. The beautiful ceramic pot we bought in 1960, the wonderful old etching with the name Phyllis on it that I got for your birthday. I find myself going around our home touching all the familiar things and crying. I know I won't start a fire, but I also know I feel like a stranger here.

Mechanically, I unpack my clothes. The bird feeder outside the French doors is empty and I fill it without thinking. These tasks keep me busy until it's time to visit you.

Tonight I am home and alone. I wander through the rooms feeling lost. Finally, I walk up the dreaded stairs. I hurry past the landing where you lay. Our bedroom is like a tomb. I don't know how I will manage to stay here. Suddenly, I jump up and pull a large carton in front of the steps. I shall take no chances.

In bed trying to sleep, I realize how much staying at Alan and Gwen's helped me. They would talk and involve me. Their kids were there or calling on the phone. The house was filled with life. I keep touching the mattress where you once lay beside me, hoping some of your warmth has remained.

PHYLLIS

❋   I keep saying "Oh, God!" and I don't even believe in God. The nurses, the patients, everyone here says, "God heals," "God has a purpose." I'm not sure there is a God. If God does exist, it is not a God of comfort.

My struggle with God began when I was seven and lying in bed in a strange cousin's house. All the important adults in my life were at the hospital. "Dear God," I prayed, "if you let my grandma live I won't play with the kids anymore. I'll make my bed. I'll dust the furniture. I'll go shopping for my grandma. I'll do anything, just make it so my grandma won't die. If she dies I'll know there is no God. I don't mean that, God. I believe in you."

In the morning I looked out the window of the fifth-floor Bronx apartment house. The sidewalks and gutters were covered with kids playing marbles. Shoe boxes and cigar boxes were everywhere. Immies, cat's-eyes, sapphires were being shot, lost, and won as far as the eye could see. It was officially marble season, after which came yo-yo season, then roller-skating season, and finally jump-rope season. My cousin and I grabbed our shoe boxes full of marbles and headed for a good curb spot. Except for lunch, we played all day and well into the sunset.

It was Friday night and my cousin, along with the rest of the world, lit the Sabbath candles. The phone rang. It was the bearer of death, my father. "Your voice is funny," I said. He replied, "Grandma is dead."

I have no comfort.

Yet, I wish I could believe. I can find no good in this accident of mine. At night I am in pain where I can feel in my shoulders, arms, and neck. I pray: *Please, if there is a God, comfort me. Take my pain and let me sleep. Help me face another day.* All I wind up doing is taking another sleeping pill. Is God a sleeping pill?

DAVID

✳ Tonight, while weight-shifting Phyllis, I tell her, "Mary and I are going to Oregon, Washington, and California. We have to do the workshops that were postponed when you got hurt."

Phyllis and I met Mary when we interviewed her for a job nine years ago. She was fresh from ending a life in New York City and ending a marriage and had almost nothing to wear as the result of a cleaning store fire that destroyed all her clothes. She was looking for beginnings, and for a job in Pennsylvania as a psychologist. We hit it off right away.

Mary is the smartest person I know when it comes to other people. She understands that people operate automatically and that it takes a hell of a crisis, a hell of an intervention, and a hell of a commitment in order to change.

Mary helped us when our kids were in trouble. Talking to them. Holding our hands. She is wonderful.

She has terrible taste in men and cars. The cars don't run but the men do.

"You have no right to leave me. I need you. I can't be without you. Damn it! I come first, not our stupid workshops."

A woman walks over to us and interrupts, "I'm Marilyn, your social worker. I'm sorry I haven't met with you but I've been on vacation." She looks sturdy and experienced. "We've scheduled your prognosis sessions with the doctor for this coming Friday. We'll tell you then about what we know about your level of injury and what we believe you can expect to achieve. Anyone who wants to come is welcome but we'd like the family there along with you, Phyllis."

"I'm going to be away for ten days. Can we do the prognosis session when I return?" David asks her.

"Yes, of course."

"I don't want to wait ten days, David."

"Phyllis, I can't postpone the West Coast trip again. Some of the money we're being paid is grant money that must be spent now. We're strapped for money at the Toughlove office. I'll ask Alan and Gwen to be here."

"Okay, okay, David, you go. Marilyn, will you please keep my appointment for Friday?"

"Sure."

On the way home tonight I feel guilty and bad, but also relieved and glad. No matter what, with this injury there are no winners.

PHYLLIS

❋ While you are gone everyone visits. Heidi brings the kids to see me today. Heidi, small, fun-loving, harassed, the middle child who tugs at my heart.

Her children, Christopher and Ian, are miniature male Heidis, freckles and blond hair. Ian, at two, is so young he seems not to notice my dilemma, but Christopher, six years old, eyes me cautiously. "He cried when he heard about your hurt," Heidi says.

Christopher asks, "Grandma, you look like a robot. Do the screws go in your head?"

"Yes, they do."

"They must hurt a lot."

"No, my dear, they don't hurt."

"Well, if they were in my head they'd sure hurt me," and he's off to play with Prince Valiant's kid.

I am grieving because Ian and Jodi's little Nitya and other children to come will never know me in a standing position and even Christopher will forget. Right now I can't even hold them. I can't stand this. My loss, my loss, dearest. I can't stand it.

Gwen, dear Gwen, like a sister to me, brings me a deli lunch which we share with the strokes and brain-injured at our table. Silent Mary of the cheese spittle dies the next day and Gwen is sure that her knish did it. I comfort her.

I think Mary would be glad, if she could be, that she is dead.

It's a good thing I've learned to like snakes, since I feel I'm turning into one. Without nerve stimulation, my skin peels off me in large sheets no matter how well I am oiled. Short circuits in my spinal nerves cause spasms that wiggle my feet, toes, and legs around like snakes before my eyes. I am cold-blooded, my thermostat no longer works. I wonder if I would like to live under a rock. "Step right up, ladies and gentlemen, see Phyllis crawl on her belly like a reptile."

✳ IX ✳

DAVID

✳ I call from Seattle as soon as I can. "Hello, Phyllis, my dear, how are you?"

"Oh, it's you, dearest. I'm so glad you called. I've been waiting and waiting. How did it go?"

"Good, but first tell me how you're doing. What's new? How do you feel? How's PT? How's wheeling? How do you feel?"

"Not too good. I have a urinary-tract infection. I have an IV with an antibiotic in it that follows me wherever I go."

"How the hell did you get the infection?"

"From the damn catheter. The nurses tell me that it happens to everybody."

"Do you have to stay in bed until you get rid of it?"

"No, the IV is on a stand with wheels. I feel like I'm a traveling circus. How did the workshop go?"

"The workshop went well. Mary and I worked at cross-purposes a few times, but that's to be expected. We'll smooth things out now that we've run through this first time. We had about fifty kids and ten parents. The kids are working and getting their lives back in order. They find the *Kid's Manual* really helpful. In fact, one of the kids said it was just like we were in his head. He hated the manual at first, but then found it was right on for what he needed. There were some problems that the parent leaders were having with the group. They didn't know how much to let the kids run things and how much control they should have. We worked it out though and I think the group will be successful."

"What hotel are you staying at?"

"We're at the Fontana Hotel. You know, the really nice one we stayed at the last time we were in Seattle."

"Yeah, don't remind me."

"I know. I miss you, my dear."

"Me too, my dear."

I hang up feeling sad. The excitement about the success of the workshop is gone. I'm just being selfish, being here while you are struggling so much. I should be there with you.

Mary, some Toughlove parents, and I go out for a great seafood dinner. The next day I'm off to California.

PHYLLIS

✳   I'm lonely with you away. I feel so hurt when you tell me about the places you and Mary go to in your time off. Places we have shared and would have again. I was looking forward to returning my hundred-dollar plastic shoes to Giorgio's. The ones where the insoles ran red. It would have been fun to do it. I'm glad the workshops are going well.

You'll be happy to know that I'm off the IV. My urinary-tract infection (called my UTI) has cleared up and the antibiotic has left me with vaginitis. My IUD is in place so life must be beautiful. I'm wheeled into PT and someone notices I don't have my IV trailing along. "Hey, Phyllis, your friend is missing." "Yeah," I say, "that fucking IV is finally gone." The place is hushed. Everyone is silent. The "F" word has their vocal chords in a state of collapse. Finally, a laugh comes up from one of the mats. It's Prince Valiant.

"Who said that?" "It's me, Phyllis," I answer unashamedly. "Well, that's great," he says. He introduces me to his wife Aleta and proudly repeats what I said.

Later I am told by my nurse that my language is a problem. It offends some of the older patients. I'm censored. But, it is right, those people can't get away from me. The community wins out over the individual. Now I have to whisper very quietly "shit" in Yiddish *(dreck)* and "fuck it" in Hungarian *(buzmek).*

A little round old man wearing a tuxedo, cummerbund, and bow tie and sporting a curling mustache saunters through the hospital like a strolling minstrel. He plays his banjo for the patients. I am wild! I am wild! I am wild with despair. I can't dance. Please save me. He makes me suffer.

He plays, "Five Foot Two, Eyes of Blue" and "Don't Sit Under the Apple Tree with Anyone Else but Me." My mother floods my memory.

She is playing the baby grand piano in our green and mahogany living room while I'm dancing. She sways to the blues she sings in her throaty contralto voice. All alone in the living room we are on stage performing. I am Ginger Rogers, Rita Hayworth, Mitzi Gaynor. My mother is Billie Holiday and all three of the Andrews sisters.

I request my favorite song, "St. Louis Blues," from the old man and tap my fingers on the arm of my wheelchair because I cannot tap my foot. My "tap dancing" tap lessons are over before they have begun. All day long I sing the blues out loud and to myself. "Now, honey, if you don't like my peaches, stop shaking my tree. Stay out of my orchard and let my peaches be."

I am singing the blues. They are in my soul, in my head, and in my life.

DAVID

❋ It's 5:30 P.M. California time. I know that visiting hours are over for you and you're in bed.

"Hello, Phyllis, how are you, my dear?"

"Oh, David, I'm so glad you called. I'm feeling terrible."

"What's wrong? Have you hurt yourself? Are you sick?"

"No, it's nothing like that. A man came and played music for us. He strolled from room to room asking what people would like to hear."

"That sounds nice, what's wrong with that?"

"I'll never dance again. I know I'm stuck forever in a wheel-chair."

Just then I heard a loud beep! beep! beep! over the phone.

"Help! Help! David. It's the fire alarm. I can't move. Oh God! don't let me burn to death."

"Phyllis! Phyllis! Relax. It's only a drill, take it easy."

"David, I'm so frightened. You know that fire is my worst fear. I can't stand the thought of scars, helplessness, and ugliness. Please! Come home."

I hear a voice in the background say, "This is only a drill. This is only a drill."

We both breathe a sigh of relief. "See, I told you it was only a drill."

"But David, what if it was for real? I'll be burned to death here, all by myself. I'm so afraid."

"Please, dear, don't worry. I'll be home in a few days. You won't get hurt anymore. Phyllis, just relax and imagine my love surrounding you. Now when you're ready, close your eyes and fall asleep protected and cradled in my love. Can you feel it now?"

Your words say, "Yes, my darling, but your message is, "Please come home."

PHYLLIS

※ Ilene, my oldest child, who stood the brunt of a mother who was almost a child herself, stands by the bed looking sad and crying a lot. Our tears mingle as I grieve for my life, my body, and the mother I was. I get angry at her tears, at her grief. I push her away. Then, as usual, I apologize. I wonder why her hurt angers me? Is it only I who can grieve? She irritates me and yet she is so good to me. It's Ilene who buys me the sweat clothes I need to wear. She searches and finds the right size and style to fit over me and my halo. It is Ilene who is here with me every weekend. It is Ilene who commutes from D. C. to Philadel-phia. It is she who loves me, who takes care of the practical. It is Ilene who still gets A's in her graduate courses.

Today Ilene and I go out for my first walk. I sit and she wheels.

It's five o'clock Friday on Halloween weekend. The traffic is fierce. I am petrified but we go anyway. Crossing the street I keep my eyes shut. I feel Ilene's effort to push and pull me. The sidewalks are bumpy and tilted; it takes all of her effort to keep me straight.

A blind man walks toward us. I think that either we'll run him over or he'll walk into us with his cane poking a hole in my foot or perhaps gouging out an eye. Ilene laughs at my frightful fantasy. We are looking for an ice cream store I can get into but we can't find any. I'm so scared. We pass a bakery but I can't get in there either. Ilene says, "Ma, I'll park you out here and I'll go in and get us something."

"I shout, "What! Are you crazy? Someone might turn my brakes and I'll fall in the gutter. A lunatic might grab my halo. Don't you dare leave me alone!"

"Okay, okay."

We hurry back to the hospital and sit in front watching traffic. Ilene buys some grapes from a Vietnamese fruit vendor. We are both out of breath and congratulating each other on how well we did. I'm almost fainting.

Going upstairs, the elevator door closes on the wheelchair and knocks the small caster wheels sideways. A good man grabs the chair and helps straighten me out. Then I get banged by the elevator door again. Ilene uses all her strength to keep the chair upright. Her face is panicked but she holds on. I think we would have died laughing if we weren't so scared and hyperventilating. Now I know what *vulnerable* is.

Out on the street I saw dirty drunks and bums on crutches. The legless and handless begging and drinking in the street. They acknowledge me, say hello, and let us pass. I used to treat drunks like this. Now they include me as part of their identity. I don't think I'll go out for a while.

"Go to the right, the left, what are you trying to do, climb the walls?"

"I can't do it," I cry.

"Yes, you can. Just a few feet to the fountain," the physical therapist says. I hit the wall and I'm stuck.

Wheeling backward seems impossible. I can't tell left from

right. I never could. I sit, I cry, I push, then sit, cry, push. A man walks up to the fountain, bends over, and takes a drink. "You son of a bitch," I snarl.

"What did you say? Are you talking to me?"

"No," and in one minute my anger propels me right to the fountain.

I guess I wasn't angry today. It took me fifteen minutes to wheel fifteen feet. I was covered with sweat, shit, and tears. I'm wearing diapers! Me! The nurses tell me not to worry. The bowel training program, enemas, a careful diet, and evacuating at a set time will take hold and I won't have any "accidents." I'm wearing diapers! Me!

Last night I dreamed I was walking up the hill to our house. I was at my slimmest and wearing the tailored tan wool jacket and skirt with the lavender blouse that was especially designed for me. I am walking and walking. I wake up crying. My legs feel as though they are wrapped around my neck. I never want to dream again.

In my life I have had some very important dreams, but one is outstanding. I dreamed I was watching the movie *Great Expectations* with Martita Hunt as Miss Haversham. At the end of the movie I walk out front, turn, and look at the marquee. The marquee says, "Great Expectations leads to Little Results." This meant to me that if I expect too much, I'll never be happy with what I get. Through my adult life I've been learning to be more content with the results of my effort. I will never be content again.

It's Halloween and Valiant has his head in a cardboard box decorated like an apple. Aleta wheels him around and he gives out apples. I have fake spiders attached to me everywhere, fuzzy ones, plastic ones, paper ones. Heidi bought them for me. I think we are all nuts. Friends come to visit me in their costumes. They sing, dance, and get rowdy.

Finally they put the make on the young man who gives out snacks. He comes in with his usual happy manner, "Anybody want anything tonight? Juice, soda, ice cream, crackers, anything I can get you?" He's the perfect host.

Out from next to my bed steps my friend Jason in drag and yells in his dishiest voice, "I'll have you, sweetie."

The snack kid turns red and never returns. My reputation will be mud.

❋ X ❋

PHYLLIS

❋   Gwen tells me my uncle calls her all the time and they have the same conversation.

"Hello?"

"Hello. Is David there?"

"No, he isn't. Who's calling?"

"It's Phyllis's uncle. How is Phyllis?"

"Doing well. As well as can be expected."

"She's walking now?"

"No. She can't walk."

"When will she walk?"

"They don't know about that yet."

"Soon? Soon she'll be walking?"

"I don't think soon."

"Is she any better?"

"Oh yes, much better."

"Good. Then she will walk soon."

"I don't think it will be soon."

"So what do they do in the hospital?"

"They work to make her stronger."

"Good. She will get stronger and then she will walk."

"They don't know if she will walk. Maybe not."

"When she gets strong."

"I hope it happens."

"Can she stand up yet?"

"No. She is paralyzed."

"When she gets strong she will stand. Then she will walk."

"I hope it happens."

"When will she be stronger?"

"I don't know. They don't have a lot of answers."

"That's the way doctors are. Soon she will walk."

"I hope so."

"You will keep us posted?"

"We'll let you know if there is news."

"You will call when she walks?"

"I'll tell David you called. I'll give Phyllis your love."

"You are a good girl."

Our family meeting with the doctor doesn't give us much new information. "The sixth and seventh vertebrae were compressed and the spinal cord was crushed. Phyllis will have some arm and hand use, but it is unlikely that she will walk. We can't say definitely, but the anterior portion of the cord received the most damage and that just doesn't mend. Medically, Phyllis is doing well and we are just waiting for a bed at the rehabilitation hospital."

We are all disappointed and hiding our feelings when the social worker attending the meeting asks, "Tell me, have you ever had anything worse happen to you?" The kids jump up in unison and yell, "What could be worse?" She stutters, "I just wondered how you coped."

No, nothing worse, but I'm thinking, everything else that has happened to me has not been physically disabling. My worst thing, being fat, can't even be compared with this. My mother's death and my father's abandonment hurt. Our daughter's arrest for robbery was excruciatingly painful and debilitating. But this is different.

I am suffering alone. No one shares the loss of this body with me. I am alone and I can't escape. Not for a second. "No, social worker, nothing worse has ever happened to me."

I know what I am. A quad! It really is a four-letter word. I'll be a "superquad," the doctor said. I will have the use of my hands, arms, and shoulders. I always did admire Wonder Woman. I can almost feel my mother lying in bed with me. When I was little and sick, she read *Wonder Woman* comics aloud to me. I became Wonder Woman alias Diane Prince and sometimes I was Etta Candy, her chubby, candy-loving secretary.

Here, at the hospital, my friends who know my past bring me comic books to comfort me, but there is no mother to lie next to me and read them aloud. They go unread.

My aunt and uncle came to see me today. This is the hardest visit for me.

My aunt and uncle have known and loved me all of my life. Their visit is painful. Perhaps because they are the closest and we share the longest history and remember everything. To them I am still a child. My aunt calls me "meine kind" (my child) and we cry. I feel even more vulnerable with them than I could ever have believed.

My beloved, I won't tell you this out loud, but only in a whisper. Last night the doctor left an empty hypodermic on my bedside table. "Ah," I thought, "my chance. I'll give myself an air bubble. So easy."

I couldn't lift the empty hypodermic. It was too heavy. My hand could not close around it and the needle rolled to the floor. I'll need someone to help me kill myself, and someone has promised. She said that if I'm this miserable, she'll help me. *I feel relieved.*

Yet another complication. I don't seem to be able to eat chocolate. Every time I put one of my dear friend Dale's lovely truffles in my mouth I start to choke. The nurses come running to help me cough. Oh, alas! Is there life after chocolate?

Dearest, I know you can't understand the ecstasy a chocolate binge brings, or the relief from the tensions of everyday life as I used to stand eating fudge straight out of a jar heating in boiling water on the kitchen stove. I have the misfortune to be married to you, who do not like chocolate even a little. What will I do with my premenstrual tension?

I will suffer every holiday. No chocolate pumpkins, or Santas, or Easter bunnies, or my favorite peanut butter chocolate eggs, no chocolate-covered matzoh, no chocolate Thanksgiving-turkey table decorations that I buy at least two of so I can eat my share before I feed them to the children. No more "some mores" at family picnics. No more bags of chocolate Kisses for emergencies in the car.

How will I ever survive a day at Bloomingdale's without their wonderful Godiva and Bloomie's chocolates, without a fresh-baked chocolate croissant?

How will I pass another Baskin-Robbins ice cream store without giving into that terrible yearning for a double-chocolate, double-scoop cone?

Perhaps there is no life after chocolate and I shall die nobly, choking on a brownie.

Every day I see dead bodies being wheeled away down the yellow corridor. I am not frightened. I think I am envious. Over the phone I tell David, "I have made a decision. I've given myself one year from the time of the accident to see what the quality of my life will be like. If I hate it I will kill myself."

"That's not enough time. You know, it's going to take one and a half to two years just for you to regain your energy. Your spinal cord will be in shock for about that time."

I am planning a murder. Last night Bessie kept her light shining in my face. I pleaded with her, "Please put your light out, it shines in my eyes."

"No, not yet," she says and falls asleep. No sooner does the nurse shut off her light than Bessie leans over and turns on her light and her radio.

"Bessie, please stop."

"Not yet, not yet," as she rummages through her bedside drawer, rattling her stash of vitamins, crackers, and prunes.

I am beginning to take her behavior personally. "This is your last chance," I scream through my tears. Bessie keeps on rummaging.

"Okay, you are dead. I just killed you. As far as I am concerned you are a dead person. You are never to speak to me or my company again. If you forget I won't answer you and neither will they. You are a dead old lady. Dead and don't forget it." Silence reigns. But her light stays on. And you, Rollo May, and you, Alfred Adler, you think you know something about power and powerlessness. Just ask me. Powerlessness leads to murder, so everyone watch your ass! Bessie is just the first.

DAVID

✳ The trip went well. Mary and I managed to work in a relatively smooth fashion. She has a "heady" and intellectual manner like me, so we worked at being warm and personal. We couldn't manage to give that extra something you always added, but what we did was well received.

I haven't seen you for a week and a half and I miss you. I meet you as you are ready to leave physical therapy. You are eager to show me something. I can't imagine what. I get behind the wheelchair to push you and you say, "No, no, go down the hall and wait." I walk the thirty feet and turn around. You have begun to follow, wheeling the chair yourself. You conquer the bump in the floor like Sir Edmund Hilary on Mount Everest. Your stronger right hand draws you to the walls as if they were magnetic. Each time you back up and start again. Eventually you make it to where I am standing, turn, and negotiate the crowded passage into your room. We are both exhausted, happy, and crying. You have gained some movement and strength in your hands and arms.

PHYLLIS

✳ I'm seeing your face after ten days. Your wonderful, tired face with the gray stubble. You look beautiful to me. I feel relieved and protected. Me, the great feminist.

You hold my hand. You touch my shoulder and I yearn to be closer to you but my hand hurts and my shoulder is tender from the exercise. I scare you away. You notice that my fingers on the left hand are beginning to move and that I am almost sitting up straight in the wheelchair. You are pleased. I'm happy to see you.

DAVID

❊ Later that night, in bed, you are crying. You tell me, "I don't want to live if I am going to be like this. David, please kill me."

"Oh Phyllis, you must live, you have to live, I don't want you to die. You're doing better, dearest. We'll be together, we'll have our safe nest." You quiet down and fall asleep.

Going home that night is devastating. Which Phyllis do I believe? The one who is straining to learn and do, or the one who wants to die?

Teresa, Gwen, and Toughlove enter our house this morning. We sit down to examine our current financial condition. Our economic position is rocky but not fatal. We agree that none of us will take any salary for the next three months.

Personally, we'll be able to make it okay, but after three months it will be iffy. I have to get back into finishing our new book, *Toughlove Solutions*. Our deadline is coming up and I don't think I can write a thing. I miss you so.

There are so many voids in my life that you fill. I need you to be with me. The wolves have gathered to tear to pieces the world we have built.

PHYLLIS

❊ Today I looked for Valiant but he wasn't around. The nurse told me he was sick. He has a UTI. I sent him, by way of the nurse, the dirtiest, funniest card I had received. He liked it even though it was used. I hope he gets better soon.

I feel so badly when you watch me in PT. I am like the legless half-a-man I once saw propelling himself down a hill in the gutter in the Bronx. He sat on a wooden platform with wheels and pushed himself with his wrists and fists. He looked dirty. I became scared and ran into my house.

I've always been a klutz and now I'm even worse. It's hard learning to walk on my wrists and push myself around the mats on my elbows. I can't stand it and I feel badly about myself doing so poorly and crying from pain. I feel even worse about having to walk on my hands. I don't want this at all.

"Phyllis, you're doing well. You've been leaning on your wrists for four minutes. Some people can't even do it for one minute," says my physical therapist.

"I thought I was awful. Please tell me, what are the goals for me anyway?"

The therapist says, "Well, the goals are sitting up straight in the wheelchair and wheeling the chair, strengthening your arms, and increasing your breathing capacity."

"What! It's a goal for me to sit up straight? I can hardly believe it. It's a goal to wheel the chair? Why didn't someone tell me? I thought I was bad because I was having so much trouble wheeling the chair and you kept pushing me to wheel." I've been trying to please and meet everyone's expectations, not even knowing what they are. I'm going to ask everyone about what my goals are.

DAVID

✳   You have been talking about this other couple for over a week. He hurt himself diving into a swimming pool and is injured as badly as you are. His workouts in PT and OT impress you greatly. He concentrates, sweats, strains, and works constantly at getting better. You told me he reminds you of a red-headed Prince Valiant. His wife is there much more often than I am. Already I am beginning to resent her.

Prince Valiant, Aleta, Phyllis, and I meet in the dining room. They are ten to fifteen years younger than we but what we now have in common transcends all other differences. All of us are hungry for the companionship of newly created equals. They have discovered the glass-enclosed lounge on the roof. What a relief to leave the four hospital-colored walls and enjoy the lights of the city at night.

I need to know how others are managing. I need to know if

Prince Valiant, like you, wants to die rather than go on. I need to know how Mrs. Valiant handles all of this. I need to know so much, but newness and unsureness about how to ask cause me to settle for pleasantries and casual conversation.

The openness of the roof frightens you, and soon we retreat back into our rooms and ourselves.

PHYLLIS

✳   Bessie's light stays out at night and she hasn't said a word to me or mine for a week.

Today I heard from my doctor that I am medically stable. My social worker tells me I'm going to Magee Rehabilitation Hospital only five blocks from here. They specialize in teaching the spinal cord injured to manage their bodies and their lives.

"You'll learn to dress yourself, handle the wheelchair, manage cooking and everything else you want to do from the wheelchair, so you can live a good life," says the social worker.

I don't believe it and I'm scared, but all I say is, "Sure."

Later the Magee psychologist whose client I will be comes to say hello.

Bessie is going to a nursing home. What will I do with my anger?

DAVID

✳   You're on the move to Magee Rehabilitation Hospital as soon as they can take you. Gwen went over and scouted the place. She brings back good reports and good news.

"The place is attractive, modern and light. The people seem really nice. You'll have your own room."

Magee is giving you privacy to help relieve your hypersensitivity to noise, lights, and movement. Everyone we ask about sensory overload tells us, "We don't know why it happens. Some people just react that way. With time the hypersensitivity will diminish." At least you will be able to get away by yourself.

I'm off again on a two-day speaking engagement. As usual, it's at a time when critical events are occurring in our life. To relieve my guilt, I have taken on the task of packing your clothes for the journey to Magee. I start out calmly enough, but I soon become a madman, putting everything anywhere. You are crying. Jodi is trying to help but is getting squashed by me. I feel like a Nazi storm trooper marching through the ghetto, but I can't stop. All my patience and tolerance have gone, leaving a frantic lunatic. Somehow, everything gets stuffed into something or other, and I drive home, exhausted.

PHYLLIS

✳ I am watching you pack my things so I can go to Magee Rehabilitation Hospital. You are acting exasperated, put upon, and annoyed. Jodi tries to help.

"Dad, I'll fold the sweat suits . . ."

"No! No! Just leave me alone. They don't crease, I'm rolling them up."

"But . . ."

"Jodi, just be quiet and get out of my way."

I enter the fray, "Jodi, come here to me. Hold Nitya up so I can see her."

"Ma, he's acting like a lunatic."

"Shh, go home, dear. It will be all right."

"Goodnight, Ma, see you at Magee."

Jodi gives David a wide-eyed look and a quick wave. David stops to give Nitya a kiss on her baby-soft cheek.

Finally everything is pushed, mashed, and mushed into green plastic garbage bags.

I am feeling guilty, bad, sad, and mad. "David, I have been worrying about your abandoning me. Tonight I want to abandon you. I'm glad you're going away tomorrow."

"Good, so am I."

"Go home, David."

As you move to the bed I see your shoulders slouch and the tightness leave your chest and I'm sorry.

"I'm just feeling nuts, Phyllis."

"Well, David, you always get nuts when you're packing. Remember how crazy you are when you get ready for a workshop or vacation. How about that time in Detroit when you left half of our stuff in the hotel?"

You laugh and say, "I'll see you at Magee."

Right now I feel good about you being away tomorrow when I move to the rehab. Gwen has arranged everything. After you left, the social worker came and gave me a black loose-leaf book. She told me the book will be filled as I progress, with the gory details of how to care for my injured body. At the rehab they will teach me to be a "good quad." I don't want to be a good quad. I want to be a whole person.

Damn it. I am going to the rehab with my period. Screwed by my body again and again.

✳ XI ✳

PHYLLIS

✳   My possessions, packed in plastic bags, crowd the ambulance. Gwen sits up front and I'm on a stretcher in the back.

It is raining and windy. The traffic is heavy. People rush across the streets holding tight to their umbrellas. I see my first tree covered in bright autumn foliage. I am surprised. My life stopped just as the trees started to turn.

At Magee, blue tile and white-and-gray walls move past me. Gwen leaves me as I am delivered to the doctor's examination room. Soon my tall, not unkind, but a little faded, jaded, callous, and badly dressed doctor examines me. He lets me know that I'll be wearing a permanent catheter called a Foley, but known as a leg bag, to pee in all my life. "It is the best thing and easiest for females with your level of injury," he says. I cry. He pats me. I think I know where my anger will go.

Meanwhile, his young female resident is standing behind him, shaking her head at me. Through the shards of my shattered self-image, I see that what the doctor is saying may not be the last word. "I'll see you later," she whispers. And she does. She tells me I can try intermittent catheterization and time voiding to train my bladder. It might take time, but it's worth it.

DAVID

✳ On my way to a teachers' convention in Atlantic City I stop to see you in your new home.

Your room is on the third floor overlooking Mole Lane, a quaint-looking street lined with old Philadelphia houses. A tree still struggling to hold on to its fall foliage is barely visible. The statue of William Penn atop City Hall completes the rest of your view.

So far the tree has impressed you most. Fall has come and almost gone, yet time stood still for you in the hospital. The color of the leaves and the dull gray look of the city in early winter remind you of real time in the real world. Lost time and lost life.

PHYLLIS

✳ The cool blue-tiled walls and halls wide enough for wheelchairs passing in the night are not friendly to me. Pillars and posts of the corridors are covered with soft gray material that is wheelchair bump-proof. The nurses' station at the end of the hallway is triangular and to me looks like the command deck of the Starship *Enterprise*. The nurses' body language demands distance on my part. They size me up with evaluative glances. They don't interact with me.

I hate the fact that you are not here with me in this newness. Instead, you are gambling in Atlantic City with a strange woman. Even if she's a journalist who has come to hear you speak at a teachers' convention, you are handsome and distinguished and I am jealous. I can feel my anger at your infidelities. I remember the scene in our Vermont living room.

You! You son of a bitch. You went to bed with that old dumpy female. You bastard, don't defend yourself. How dare you say punching, scratching, and hair-pulling isn't fair? What the hell is this? Are we playing by the Marquis of Queensberry's rules?

Sure, sure, I know you love me. It'll be all right. I just have to get this out of my system, you son of a bitch.

Fifteen years it took us to get our sex life together. My own body-hatred stood in the way. Your unshared fantasies, so pleasurable to you, pushed me away, but we fought it out and won.

I have come to accept that you are separate from me and can hurt me.

I am afraid again. Every new place is a trauma for me. The strangeness and largeness of the place makes me feel so small. It's funny because I have always felt too large for life especially on the South Bronx train I rode to school. At every stop it became more crowded with small Puerto Rican men in pink shirts. I towered above them. There wasn't enough room for me. As I hung from a strap, swaying with the rhythm of the train, my high heels killed my feet, my blue linen dress was crushed and plastered to my body from the summer heat. My feet swelled out of my shoes. My bust crept out of my neckline; my legs were so large, my skirt hiked up. As the train got more crowded, I felt that I was growing larger and larger.

In this strange place I look into the mirror above my sink. I see my image—hair, dark and trapped under a halo; a white face lifted up and held back by a brace. All I need is a feather stuck in my halo and I'd see an American Indian. My high cheekbones betray my Slavic heritage.

DAVID

✳ Magee is much more pleasant than the rehab floor at Jefferson. Here, at Magee, the wide space, the guards at the entrance, and the newness is comforting. They're strict about visitors and visiting hours. I get a badge and wait until it's time to go up.

The elevator is big enough to take at least four wheelchairs, with buttons strategically placed so that people in wheelchairs can reach them. It gives me an inkling about how much our home will have to be changed for you. Walking down the hall of the third floor where you are staying, I pass a rec room with a pool table in it and a lounge with a large color TV set. The nurses' station, down at the end of the hall past your room, is surrounded by a waist-high counter with some nurses bustling about while others sit there writing in the patients' charts. The place has an atmosphere of competence and efficiency.

Entering your room I find you in bed looking exhausted.

"How are you, my dear?" I bend over and gingerly kiss you in the space outside the halo.

"I'm okay. I just feel so tired all the time. I don't have any energy. How are you, dearest, and how was Atlantic City?"

Sitting down beside your bed I try to hold your hand, but you quickly pull your hand away, letting me know that your hands are still painful to the touch. I settle for words. "I feel pretty good. The workshop had about seventy-five teachers and administrators in it. Their reactions and questions were very encouraging. Several folks stayed after the talk was over and wanted to know how to use some of the Toughlove ideas in the classroom. There were two people who quietly asked me how they could get in touch with a Toughlove group for themselves.

"I was interviewed on the school network radio. We did a taping they plan to play some time next month. I think it went really well. The interview with the reporter was a good one. You would probably like talking to her. She has written one book about a mass murderer and is writing another. When I told her how you liked to read about mass murderers she said she'd send a copy of her book. Also, if you're up to it, she would like to come to the hospital and interview you. I said I would ask you. What do you think?"

"I don't want to be interviewed or even seen by anybody. It's hard enough being here like this without talking to strangers about my life." As you say this you begin to cry and I feel like a thoughtless fool.

"I'm sorry. I didn't think. I'll call her up and tell her she can't come."

"David, I don't want this life. I hate it! There are no redeeming features to it at all. I'm just a burden to everyone. I just want to die. Besides, I'm jealous of her."

"C'mon, Phyllis, I love you, you silly poop. Anyway, you just got here. Things will get better. We'll make a life. At the very least we'll have each other and a home. We'll write, the kids will come. Just go to sleep now."

As I leave I tell you, "Sleep cradled in my love," and I kiss you lightly on your tear-stained cheek.

I call you when I get home, to help with the pain I'm feeling. The conversation is slightly more upbeat this time. "David," you say, "sleep cradled in my love," reassuring me.

PHYLLIS

✳ My first weekend at Magee I am bloody, nauseated, and fainting. "Your period is very heavy. We've never seen one like it," comments one of the nurses. "I've never seen one like it either," I say. "I think it's the blood-thinner I'm taking for blood clots." Dr. Marx blames me, not the blood thinner. He thinks I'm crazy, and I begin to doubt myself. My own medical, pharmacological, anatomical, biological knowledge is minute. Then I think, whose body is this anyway?

You, my beloved, are scared. You tilt my chair backward to stop me from blacking out. I love you. Soon you are going to leave me for a workshop in Virginia. Who will tend me then?

At night I dream of the blue, bloody pajama bottom of my first period. I see my mother in her bedroom, in the early-morning white-window-shade dark; she's lying in bed with her head on three pillows.

"Ma, I think I have my period."

"Oh, no," she says quietly and her eyes water and her face grows a little red. She gets up on her elbow and smacks me right across my face.

"To keep the color in your cheeks." She explains the superstition as if nothing had happened. I'm in shock. We go into the bathroom where she teaches me to use a belt with a pin that will stick into me and a Modess pad that will crawl up my backside and leave the crotch of my panties bloody.

DAVID

✳ My visits are like trips to the morgue. You are pale and barely able to move. I spend most of my time tilting your head back and your legs up, trying to coax the blood out of your useless lower body and into your working head and arms. I had thought this phase would end when we left Jefferson.

"Dearest, I'm sorry to leave you now, you seem so weak. It's hard to go. I asked the kids to be sure they visit."

"I'll be okay."

I'm off again for my last trip before Thanksgiving. Leaving you now is hard. You're so weak and undefended. I have asked our kids and friends to be sure and visit. As usual, I hate the feelings of relief that go with getting away from the situation for a while.

The next evening I call Magee and Phyllis tells me, "I'm getting my energy back along with my weekly rehab schedule. Physical therapy every morning, occupational therapy every afternoon. Group therapy and a spinal cord injury class once a week. I also have meetings with a social worker and a psychologist. They are encouraging us to go out on weekends. Oh my God, I think, where can we go?

"My social worker brought me articles and books about people who have survived this trauma, but I can't look at them. Will you do it?"

"Of course I will."

"My psychologist and I are just getting acquainted. She is in her mid-twenties, newly married, and attractive. She wears lovely antique jewelry. I asked her about the brace on her leg and the crutch she uses. 'I had polio when I was a kid, she told me.' "

"What else did she say?"

"I didn't ask her the real question, 'How will I live this way?' "

"You will! I'll take care of you! I'll build us a nest! And we have each other."

PHYLLIS

❋ The PT room is bright and large. The sounds and sights are familiar to me. People trying to move, therapists cheering them on with encouraging words: "Come on, you can do it, you almost got it that time. Breathe, breathe, you can turn over; push, push. I'm here; I won't let you fall." Sometimes chiding: "Come on, don't be lazy; you need to work harder." And patients' old familiar strains, "I can't do it, I'm too tired. That's too hard. You work me too hard," and on and on.

Claire, my physical therapist is blonde, beautiful, and very professional. She explains not only how to work my muscles and how to exercise, but *why* I'm doing it. She tells me what my triceps will do for me later when I need to be more independent. She's going to teach me how to use a transfer board to get in and out of the wheelchair. She'll show my family how to move me around, especially in and out of cars in my halo. "You'll learn a lot and will became much more independent than you think you'll be," she reassures me, "but it will take time for your body to adjust to your injury. There's no way to predict how long that will be. You just have to keep working." How long? A year or more? *Independent,* that word sticks in my mind.

A woman rolls onto the mat next to mine and starts to work out. I can tell that she has an old injury. She is dressed in street clothes, not sweats, and she doesn't have the shocked, glazed look of all of us newly hurt.

At first glance she looks like the kind of woman who can be big and beautiful, flamboyant like an actress, larger than life.

"Hello, who are you? I'm Phyllis."

"That's funny, my name is Philomena," she says.

"What happened to you?"

"I tried to move my desk at work and injured my spinal cord. The sons of bitches paid dearly. My husband walked out on me, that bastard." This last sentence scares me.

"What are you in for now?" I ask, as if she's doing time.

"I'm going to walk again. Some place is going to do right by me. I was in Moss three times and they said they couldn't help me so I got myself in here," she says.

"How long ago did your accident happen?" I pushed on. Then it came.

A lifting of the eyebrows, the eyes closing to a slit, the lips pulled downward; a slight pause, the open mouth sucks in air and a little machine-gun tremor starts somewhere in the back of her throat. "I've been in THE CHAIR," pause, "for three years now." Quietly to herself, as though she's received a stage direction from an unseen playwright, she repeats, "three years now," and looks at me.

"My," I say, "what long fingernails you have [the better to scratch your eyes out] and so well manicured. I love your polish. It's divinely purple."

"I used to do a little typing to make a couple of dollars, and I took piano lessons to strengthen my hands. I kept breaking my nails so I stopped," she says.

"Claire, Claire," I call my PT. "What else should I do? I've finished trying to breathe."

"Next, we'll try balancing on the edge of the mat." That's what I need. Perfect, I think. I can't talk when I'm balancing. I can really understand the need for glamour in THE CHAIR. Will I become cure-seeking, more bitter and vain than I am now? I'm frightened.

At the weight-lifting class, therapists disguised as pep-rally leaders set a smart pace for their pupils, who can barely hold their heads up, let alone lift a weight. Most of us use one-, two-, or three-pound weights Velcroed to our wrists because we cannot grip anything. I'm one of the lucky ones. My grasp is returning. If we can do three repetitions in a row without fainting or hyperventilating, we're happy. Our PT cheerleaders get the best workout.

In OT I work to strengthen my hands and gain dexterity. I squash, pull, and generally mangle putty to exercise my hands. I draw and paint, too. All I can put on paper is that which offends my psyche—wheelchairs and crippled limbs. I am so offended. I'm told that typing is great for my hands so I'll need to do a lot of it. Ugh!

Here I see people who have no visitors to bring their laundry home to wash with loving care. They use the washing machine in occupational therapy to clean their clothes. I cannot imagine how they manage.

I hate the Magee dining room. It's set up cafeteria style, with helpers to assist us. The food is greasy and awful. As you know, dearest, I wouldn't wait on line if the Pope himself was serving manna from heaven, so why should I wait here?

But the truth is, I just can't manage it. The lights are too bright, the painted orange walls too garish, and the people on prone carts scare me. At first I thought these guys lying on their stomachs had no lower bodies and I wanted to run away but couldn't. Now, I always have to stay and fight. So I asked a nurse, "Who are these people lying belly-down on carts that they wheel around with their arms?" She told me they are mostly young paraplegic guys who had skin breakdown, bedsores gone rampant. Many had plastic surgery on their buttocks and they are here to heal and learn skin care. The rumor is that a lot of the guys are macho and want to be cool, so they refuse to weight-shift. They pretend that they don't need special care. They do a lot of dope outside on the patio.

I will not go to the dining room. I have asked Teresa to bring me cold cereal, instant hot cereal, peanut butter, instant soup, and crackers. If I can get milk from the nurses' station, I'll be set for the daytime. At night, I'll ask you all to bring me dinner or order out.

I am too tired to enjoy visitors at night. Me, the social butterfly. I realize how much I used to entertain people. I don't have that entertainment energy left anymore. How boring I am.

⁕ XII ⁕

PHYLLIS

⁕ Alone in my room darkness grabs my heart. I am besieged by permanent, never-ending neck and shoulder pain. I hear a noise. A nurse is in my room. Actually it is her room. I, the patient, am only a guest passing through her house. In the mirror I see a tall, pretty young woman pat her sweater, fix her hair, examine her eyes, wrinkle her nose while gazing fixedly at her image.

She sees me in the background of her reflection. Does she see an old lady? Is she curious about me? Does she think, Oh, here is the forty-six-year-old spinal cord in Room 343. I'll bet she's a real winner, someone who is going to complain and cry. I'll shape her up.

"You look great," I say meekly. Quickly she turns, smiles, and says, "I'm Di. I'll be your regular nurse. I'll be teaching you bowel, bladder, and other elements of body care. If you have any questions or need anything, please ask me. I'll be with you every day from three to eleven."

I say to myself, What is she saying? I need someone every second to touch me, blow my nose, wipe my ass, pat my hand, sit me up, lie me down. I need someone to teach me to live or die. Can this young woman do all this?

Out loud I say, "How old are you?"

"Twenty-six. I hear you are famous," she says.

I wonder to myself if spinal cord injury makes you famous or has she found out what a great wimp I am already.

"Don't you write?"

"Oh, yes. I run a national organization called Toughlove and I write." I want to yell, "And I love clothes, travel, life, walking, dancing, and holding babies in my arms. I want to turn the clock back. I don't want to be here. Can you help me?" But I don't. I'm still on good behavior.

"Do you need anything?" she says as she almost runs out the door in her sneakers, which are always wet from showering patients.

"No."

"I'll be back with your pills soon."

I go back to my darkness and pain.

Later she is back in the mirror again, pulling and pushing at her hair. "I don't think you like the way you look," I blurt out in my usual style.

"Why do you say that?" Di's mirror image asks.

"Well, you seem to rearrange yourself every time you walk in." I didn't add that I recognize my own self-hatred.

"I'm fat; I need to go on a diet," this tall thin person says.

In my most casual voice I ask, "How do you survive this?"

"You'll learn. You'll see. We'll help you. You'll get stronger. You'll be able to manage your body."

I want to say, "Will I look better?" but I don't say it yet. I'm afraid to hear her answers.

"Look at Jim down the hall. He goes out at night over the weekend. His friends come and they go to bars. He's registering for school. Sure he's scared, but he's doing it. You'll know how to do a lot by the time you leave. Just keep working at it." Di is comfortable with this "it will be better" speech and is oblivious to its effect on me. I look at her in astonishment and disbelief. Di turns around, laying screeching rubber on the tile floor, and is gone.

*

"Oh, my God. I can't stand this. I want to die," I whisper and cry to myself.

Suddenly she's back, her hand on my shoulders. "It really will get better. Give us a chance, okay?"

"Okay," I say. I think I like her.

DAVID

* "The life-size wooden cow I bought for your birthday has been stolen. Someone just took it off our lawn. I've been so distracted I never noticed it was missing. I feel so badly losing another piece of our life that was pleasurable." I am frightened and angry at my defenselessness and at others' greed.

PHYLLIS

* I love to see cows hanging out in stony Vermont fields. Fog hovering before the morning sun.

I love to see cows, fresh from spending a long winter stanchioned in the barn. Black and brown cows. Brown and fawn-colored cows, lying in a big pile under the few elms left on the Vermont hillside. I love to stand on the hilltop and look out at small dots down the hill that are black and white cows in a Grandma Moses painting.

"I'm sorry it's gone. How mean people are." But I'm glad you're back.

DAVID

* Tonight Prince Valiant and Ike, the injured football player, are in your room when I come to visit. It is like old home week. The two of you are busy telling Ike war stories about life at Magee. Ike has just arrived from Jefferson and is happy to find you two waiting for him. The room is filled with good feelings. I am amazed at the camaraderie we have all developed so quickly. The legion of the crippled offers instant brotherhood.

Ike asks about the family room. "Have you seen it? What's it like? How do you get to use it?"

I tell him, "You need to ask your social worker to sign you up. Maybe you need your doctor's approval. I don't know."

"Me either," says Valiant.

The family room is a small apartment designed to give the injured person and his or her partner a place to practice home living, but primarily to try out sex.

Ike is anxious to spend the night with his girl friend, May. Valiant, you, and I grow silent. Sexuality and sex are scary landscapes where we fear to tread. I'm sure that Ike and May are seeking that impossible dream: "normal." We each try to slow Ike down.

"Listen, Ike, it's sort of early," Valiant says. "Maybe you should wait until the halo comes off."

"Ike, I think May needs some time to get used to Magee," you say.

"Yeah, Ike, give yourself some time. You just got here, too," I say.

"Well, May and I want to try it. It can only get better when the halo comes off."

"It's your ball game," quips Valiant.

I envy Ike's enthusiasm. I wonder about our own hesitancy. Sex seems so out of reach right now. Will it ever become part of our life again? I gently pat your arm, avoid your eyes, and turn to tell you, "I just received our editors' comments about our book. We need to go over them and decide how to respond." Valiant and Ike take the cue and leave. "I want your moderating influence on my tendency to get preachy and intellectualize. I'm worried about our deadline if I delay too long."

"David, please put me in bed. I'm in a great deal of pain across my neck and shoulders." I put you in bed and turn you over on your side, spread out the papers, and begin. "Phyllis, there are a couple of comments here that we really have to discuss. The editor wants us to rethink some of our ideas on suicide."

"David, dear, I'm sorry, will you fix the pillow?"

"Sure," and I move the pillow so that your neck is better supported.

"Listen to this. She says here that . . . "

"Will you raise my legs?"

*   *   *

"Sure," and I crank up your legs. "You've got to pay attention, Phyllis. We really need to work on the book."

"I'm sorry, David, but could you just turn me over again? My neck and shoulders are killing me."

"Okay, but then pay attention to me a little bit, will you?"

"I'll try, but first can you get me a drink of water?"

"Will you ask the nurse to check my blood pressure?"

"Will you fix the pillow?"

I feel awful. How could I even think you could respond? What is wrong with me that I won't accept that your life, thought, and energy belong to the hospital now? What the hell does the book matter when your very existence is so painful?

Later I telephone for our usual just-before-bedtime conversation. Your phone is picked up and a long series of sounds, banging, knocking, grunts, and groans ensue, until I hear your breathless "Hello." In my mind's eye I picture the physical exertion and contortion you go through to do the simple task of putting the phone on your pillow next to your ear. Your hands don't have the strength to hold it. Your pain is worse and you are too tired to fight it anymore.

"David, I want you to stop saying and thinking, 'If only I had asked you if you were all right that night.' It's over with. I can no longer be saved. Stop telling me, 'I'll build you a nest, a safe place. At least we'll have each other and a nice house.' I don't want you to love me, David. I don't deserve it. I have nothing to give you anymore. I am garbage. The first to go into the oven. David, please kill me. I can't go on."

"Hang in there my dearest," I say. "You'll feel better in the morning. Don't give up now. The worst is behind us." I go on and on, hoping to evade the horror or your request. I change the subject, talk about our kids, our grandchildren, our friends, anything. But you won't be distracted.

"David, I can't go on. If you love me you will kill me."

I end up doing what I'm best at: withdrawing. "I have to hang up now. Goodnight, my dearest, and sleep cradled in my love!"

"David, you have got to kill me. Life is not worth it anymore!"

"Go to sleep, Phyllis, you'll feel better in the morning. I'll see you tomorrow. Goodnight." You persist longer than usual tonight but eventually release me with a tearful goodnight.

I lie in bed feeling terrible. I understand your desire to die. I know I would feel the same in your place. I am obligated to and responsible for you. It is up to me to make sure your life is as good as it can be.

I hate what has happened to us, but I will not let go of you and our life. I hate your asking me to end it. I can't hate you. There is enough self-hate in you without my adding to it.

Eventually, I fall asleep.

—— ✳ XIII ✳ ——

PHYLLIS

✳ I hear my own voice, "Why should I want to live? How will I stand this broken life? This terrible life?" The tears are streaming down my face.

The newly injured and the long-ago-hurt in this counseling group are staring at me. Most of the men, like me, can't move, so they are not squirming. One young kid picks this moment to black out. A nurse/counselor tips his wheelchair back so his blood pressure can rise.

"How can you live?" I insist. "Tell me." Finally a male outpatient speaks. "My name is Carl and I've been like this for twelve years." In my mind I have already negated him. He can cross his legs and he carries crutches on the back of his wheelchair. "For the first eight years I drank myself into oblivion and self-pity," he continues. Uh, oh, I know a good A.A.-er when I see one, I think. I've heard this story in one form or another a million times. The next line will be about finding his higher power and how he now has a good relationship with his family. I tune back in to hear him say, "I couldn't believe I was getting around Wanamaker's doing my Christmas shopping."

Twelve years, twelve damn years. I can't wait that long to go to

Bloomingdale's. Later, Valiant comes to my room. "Phyllis, you mean a lot to me. You are worthwhile, if that means anything to you. Please live." David, you are quiet, but you pat Valiant's shoulder and whisper, "Thank you."

We are going out this weekend. "It's good for you," the entire staff of Magee insists. I don't want to go, I'm too scared. My fate in the form of a pass for Saturday and Sunday is at the desk signed and sealed by Dr. Marx.

"Phyllis, are you ready to go? It's cold out, but I've brought my heavy sweater to put you into. Give me your arm, there, now sit forward a little, I'll pull it down in the back. It's perfect, here's my scarf." You babble as you stuff me into the clothes and wheel me out to pick up the pass. This must be how nursery kids feel as their parents and teachers dress them.

"Oh good, you're going out," the nurses are so pleased. "Have a good time; be back by eight; don't forget your pills," all my mothers chatter at me.

"I'm only going across the street to the hotel for a drink with Valiant and Aleta."

"Oh, going out, that's great!" Even the elevator operator is thrilled to see me go. "Going home, eh?"

"No, I'm just going across the street to the hotel."

A little disappointment is in his voice. "Why aren't you going home?"

"It's too far to go," I respond.

"Well, well," says the guard at the desk, "Mr. York, I'm glad to see you bringing your lady out, have a good time. You going home?"

"Nope," David answers as he starts to put on my gloves, stuffing every little piggy into the right hole. "Oh," he mutters. Another person we have let down.

"Next time I guess," the guard says. "Have a good time anyway."

"Isn't it nice out even though it's cold, Phyllis?"

"I don't know. I'm scared, don't push me so fast. How will we cross the street?"

"Not to worry, watch this." You've let go of the wheelchair. "See, no hands," you say. I'm hyperventilating and crying. "I've got you," you tell me. "I'm just trying to show you how safe you really are."

"Wah!" I'm hysterical.

"I'm sorry. I didn't mean to scare you." The light changes and we cross the street and go into the hotel. A sci-fi convention is being held here. Everyone is running around in surreal costumes. Some of them actually come up and talk to Valiant and me in the bar. They are so far out they think we're in costume, too. We tell them we're twins from the planet Zip. We laugh, but I'm still so scared and overwhelmed by everyone and everything that I can scarcely breathe. I spend a lot of time weight-shifting on David's lap, like a nursing child running for mamma when feeling hurt and afraid.

Back at Magee my very own steady nurse has just appeared after four days of invisibility. "I bet you thought you'd never see me again," Di says.

Wide-eyed, I coolly say, "I didn't think about it" (liar, liar, house on fire).

"Di, this is my husband, David."

"Hi, David. I'm Phyllis's regular nurse. I'll teach you, and anyone else who would like to learn, how to help Phyllis care for herself." Di talks as though a large audience were present. "I'd like to suggest that you go to our spinal cord injury class. Tonight's session is on skin care."

"Okay," David says stoically.

"If you have any questions, please feel free too ask," Di bubbles.

"I will, thank you," David responds politely.

"David, if I am going to Gwen and Alan's for Thanksgiving, you have got to make time to learn how to transfer me in and out of our car. Otherwise I can't go."

"I know, I know," a harassed David answers.

"You don't want to come and see me in PT do you, David?"

"No, damn it. I don't have time to do everything. I'm up to my eyeballs in things that need doing now. I'm so burdened."

"I'm sorry," I say, crying again.

"I have to go to the spinal cord injury class, Phyllis. I'll see you later."

"David hates who I am now. David hates me," I tell Valiant while David and Aleta are in class.

"Aleta can't stand me talking about myself all the time," confides Val. "She doesn't realize what this is like."

I am distracted by a slight movement in Valiant's left hand. "Your fingers are moving. That's new. How wonderful!" Off we go talking about what works. What doesn't work. How PT and OT are going. The condition of our bowels and bladders. Just the normal run-of-the-mill rehab self-centeredness.

Visiting hours and the class end at the same time. "How was it, David?" No answer. "How was it, David?"

"Scary. They showed us terrible movies of bed and pressure sores. I still don't know what to do to prevent them. It was awful."

I find myself again saying, "I'm sorry," and then I add, "Maybe you should talk to Di about what to do."

"Not now, not now. Where's your dirty laundry?" David rushes for a task to avoid what's happening. "Oh, I see it. I'm going. I'll call you later." David's exit with two large bags of dirty clothes leaves me feeling scared.

Lady Di gets me ready for a shit and a shower. She sits me on the edge of the bed. Helped by Myra, a drill sergeant disguised as a nursing assistant, she gets ready to throw me into the horrible potty-shower chair. Suddenly Lady Di laughs and yells out, "Oh, my God, your legs are too short to reach the floor." Her humor heals me.

"It's okay, I don't have to walk anymore," I reassure her. "Maybe when the halo comes off they will grow." We laugh.

Later over the phone, it is easier for me to listen to David's pain and loneliness. He cradles me in his love. I am sorry for the self-centeredness that ensures my survival. I love you and hate you.

DAVID

❋ The "Spinal Cord Injury Class for Spouses and Friends" is a disaster. The main attraction is a gruesome film. Bedsores are shown that have taken over possession of all kinds of rear ends. Bones protruding from gaping wounds and oozing fluids are shown in living color. Now I know what is under those bed-sheet tents covering people on prone carts. Oh, my poor dear, is this what your unrepentant bedsore will lead to?

The lecture presents the dynamics of bedsores. Bone pressure, blood pooling, skin breakdown, all due to unrelieved pressure. The cure? Doing a weight shift every twenty to thirty minutes. "But we do that and Phyllis still has a bedsore."

"Do it better."

"How?"

"Make sure you are relieving the pressure. Make sure the patient gets off her behind, or knee, or hip, or ankle. Wherever the bone protrudes to cause blood pooling."

"We do that now but Phyllis can't get rid of her bedsore."

"Do it better."

Catch-22, I feel your sting. I prefer my disasters be spontaneous.

The next day Lady Di comes in and begins to bustle about. I ask her what she thinks is causing your continuous bedsore. A lengthy lecture ensues on spinal cord injury and its mysterious effect on skin. Lady Di is a treasure chest of information and believes in covering every detail exhaustively. I need her knowledge. In the process of her thesis on skin care and spinal cord injury, Lady Di asks me if I have read the "black book." When I profess ignorance, she dashes off and returns with a massive black loose-leaf book. It is to be our bible, she informs us. It provides all the information about body care and the supplies we will need.

Nurse Di believes that I should know how to do every task that the nurses do for you. I tell her that I want to learn. "We are determined to be as independent as possible," I say in my most righteous manner.

"Most people don't want to get involved," she says. "The wearying constancy of care erodes the fabric of a relationship until the injured person is left alone." I couldn't imagine myself feeling that way. But I fear the possibility. I refuse to let that happen to our love. She shows me how to clean your bedsore. Di is a good teacher.

It is a thoughtful, painful ride home that night. I push aside my doubts. I won't recognize the relief I feel when I go away on business trips. We will make it work. I will never abandon you. I know my commitment, but I question my resolve and stamina.

Sleep is a stranger tonight.

The next day, Hal, who has drifted in and out of our lives since we worked together at Eagleville Hospital, calls and invites me out to lunch. I quickly agree and we meet at a restaurant in New Hope. He is a gentle, thoughtful person whose clothes have a mind of their own. Shirttails quickly work their way free, pants hike up and sag at whim while Hal's ministrations prove fruitless. The years have left him resigned and impervious to the sartorial rebellion that rages upon him.

"How are you, David? How are you managing?"

He refuses to accept my evasive response of, "Fine, thanks. How about you, Hal?"

"No, David, I mean really, how are you? I can see that Phyllis has plenty of attention and help, but what about you?"

Cornered, I reach for the painful truth. "I'm tired and frightened, Hal. I'm also angry as hell that this terrible accident has happened to us. I divide my time between work, the hospital, and our new book. None of it seems very rewarding now." Hal hugs and pats me in the way of men while I struggle to hold back the tears in the way of men.

Hal says, "Look, David, I know that now is not the best time, but I have some information about this Dr. Brucker's research in biofeedback and spinal cord injury. He is doing some unique and pioneering work. He doesn't believe that the spinal cord doesn't continue some kind of regeneration. He's a very exciting man. Hang on to it and read it when you have time." He hands me a sheaf of papers which I stuff away for later. "Thanks, Hal, I appreciate your caring." The sheaf of papers seems like another burden I don't need.

PHYLLIS

❋ David's come with an article given him by Hal on spinal cord injury and biofeedback.

Our friend Hal is a fortyish, chubby, shirt-tails-out-like-a-little-kid, Freudian, bearded psychologist. He introduced me to working with drug addicts and alcoholics at Eagleville Hospital and Rehabilitation Center, where I was a therapist. His slow speech belies his quick wit and sharp intelligence. But his outstanding feature is his kindness. Perhaps he is in touch with suffering. We give the article to Dr. Marx and he says, "This may work with an incomplete injury, but not you." We are again disappointed and hopeless. "You are complete. If you had some sensations below your level of injury, we would know your spinal cord was not completely crushed, but you don't have any sensations. You will not benefit from Dr. Brucker's work."

Every day David lugs away from the hospital shopping bags filled with dirty clothes. Every day he comes in with shopping bags filled with clean clothes. I have made a shopping-bag lady out of him.

One day, when I was a kid, I watched my mother walk down to where my friends and I hung out on the stoop of our building. Her shopping bags weighed her down. Her skinny legs in short boots stuck out from under her oversized gray Persian lamb coat as she waded through the slushy winter-snow-filled city gutter.

Startled out of my "glamorous entertainer" childhood dream image of her, I felt embarrassed and ashamed and angry at her.

"Phyllis, Phyllis, come help me," she calls. "Phyllis," she's demanding.

I take a bag from her, lifting it into my arms. "Why don't you hold it by the handles? That's what they are for," she says.

"I'll never carrying shopping bags when I'm married. They're disgusting."

With a mother's wish turned curse my mother says, "I hope you won't have to, Lady Godiva."

Forgive me, David.

"David, please comfort me."

"I'm trying, Phyllis."

"Hold my hand, lie in bed with me. Hold me. Touch me," I plead.

"Whenever I held your arm or hand before, it hurt."

"But that was a long time ago. I think you don't want to touch me, that I am too horrible to touch and you hate me."

"No, don't be foolish. Of course I love you. I don't want to hurt you," you say in such a loving voice that I believe you for a moment.

"How the hell can I know what to do if you don't tell me? I can't mind-read," you add.

I'm crying and crying, "You're always nasty. I think you hate to come here."

"No, I don't, but it's hard. I'm doing everything. Then I have to come here and I'm never doing the right thing."

"Don't come every day. I can't stand it. I don't enjoy your visits, not when they're like this. You are so harassed and I feel guilty. David, will you please get me out of bed?"

"Okay, but then I have to talk to you about the book."

"All right, just get me up. I can't stand lying here another minute."

Fifteen minutes of lifting, pulling, pushing, arranging feet, legs, clothes, and body.

"Are you comfortable now?"

"Please fix my cushion."

"All right?"

"Yeah."

"Phyllis, listen, I've made a decision about the book. I'll write it myself. I don't think our editor will like everything but I'm going to do it my way."

"David, could you fix my leg, please?"

"Phyllis, do you hear me?"

"Of course, I'm just so uncomfortable."

"Okay, what do you think?"

"Please get me a drink, David."

"Can't you pay attention to me and what I need for two minutes? This is important."

"I can't. What do you want from me? I think what you're doing is right."

"I want you to get out of yourself and listen to me, damn it."

"I try, but I can't. Do what you want. David, don't come here every day. I can't stand you to visit me. I think you just come because you should. I don't need this. I can't give you what you want."

"It's hard for me too, Phyllis. I want to be here; when I'm not I can hardly stand it."

"Please don't come all the time."

"We'll see."

We are such a disappointment to each other.

No matter how hard I try I can't get into Toughlove. I have no passion left for anything.

✳ XIV ✳

DAVID

✳   Working at Goddard College in the sixties had been an exhilarating and freeing experience for me. The college didn't offer required courses or grades. Instead, I and other teachers would make up learning contracts with the individual students, which teacher and student would evaluate at the end of the semester. I was required to be a counselor for twelve to fifteen students, to help them over the tough job of adjusting to the personal freedom the college offered.

By trying to get young people to talk about themselves, I learned that it was okay to talk about me. By living in an atmosphere that encouraged self-expression, I learned to express me, not just the uptight, rigid, isolated me but the caring, feeling, and crazy me as well.

The problem with all this exciting, fun stuff was that I wanted it all for myself and I didn't want Phyllis with her blunt candor and intuitive insights interfering. I feared she would say something or do something that would ruin my image as the bright, wonderful teacher and daddy to all. This was especially important in the adoring, seductive interactions that some young people give to teachers. I didn't want any of the reality of father, husband, and inadequate male getting in the way of these delicious fantasies.

Fortunately, Phyllis was not the kind of person to sit idly by and become increasingly isolated by my behavior. She made friends with other faculty wives, became a student at the college, and displayed the wonderful gregarious talent that she has and I so sorely lack. As we began talking to and about students together I was constantly surprised at her insight and ability to talk directly. These were foreign talents to me and my desire to learn them became more important than my need to keep my fantasy life alive and well. We had been married for ten years but for the first time I became genuinely interested in this woman I had married. But I didn't give up my fantasy life easily; it took at least another ten years and several affairs to accept that the life and wife I had was the life and wife I wanted.

When we considered working at Eagleville Hospital and Rehabilitation Center as drug and alcohol counselors, we knew that the therapeutic community atmosphere of the hospital had the same excitement and intense personal involvement as at Goddard. We realized that we needed to be working in the hospital together if our marriage was going to remain intact. By working together, we became more and more supportive and committed to each other. Working and living together made our marriage even better and stronger. When we left Eagleville we knew that we wouldn't find another job that would allow us to continue the closeness that we had developed, so we started our own consulting and training business.

Writing business proposals together, traveling around the state of Pennsylvania together, and seeing our plans become realities made our relationship even stronger. We became business partners, best friends, and lovers all in one.

But this—this injury. It is inexorably driving a wedge between us. I've lost my anchor and feel as though a gale is pushing me away from you.

"Phyllis, listen to this last chapter, okay?"

"Please fix my foot."

"Phyllis, you don't care about me and our work."

"I feel terrible about your pain, but I'm also very angry."

"For Christ's sake, Phyllis, I know you hurt but we also have other things going on. Our business, this book, and my life count. Can't you ever get out of yourself for five minutes?"

By now we are both crying.

"No, I can't. I just want to die. I can't give you anything. Kill me! Kill me! Kill me! That's all I want and all I can think about."

"Phyllis, I won't do that. I can't do that and live with myself. Stop asking."

PHYLLIS

✳   A knock on the door and my new woman friend and counselee/counselor enters. It's Jennnifer. She comes raw from a terrible car crash that killed her lover and damaged her spine. She knows she'll be able to walk and, with exercise, regain the use of her arms. She mourns the loss of her lover and her body. She grieves for her life, barely started at twenty-one.

Jennifer keeps me company. She sometimes steals into my room late at night after smoking a joint with some prone cart prisoner. She's mellow and listens to my suicide talk. I help her sort out what is and what may come. The intensity of her feelings in this drama are still unreal to her. I give her what I can't give David.

Jennifer, like all of us, looks tired and disheveled. The leather brace holding her neck in place makes her sigh with pain.

"David, this is Jennifer." I'm trying to pull myself together.

"Hi," you say as you cooly turn away to fix my sheet.

"Well," Jennifer says, edging toward the door, "I'll see you later."

The quad down the hall has stopped by to say hello, too.

"David, this is Lloyd."

"Hi," you say.

We gossip, "Did you see the new kid? He's a para."

"Wasn't OT freezing today?"

"David, Lloyd is another diving catastrophe." So many necks are broken diving into pools.

You just shake your head.

"I'm going to supper," says Lloyd.

"See you," and he leaves.

Then, the drill sergeant arrives to take my blood pressure. We talk about the weight-lifting and the body-building she does.

"What's her pressure?" you ask.

"Ninety over sixty," she says on her way out of the door.

"David, I'm sorry, I just can't pay attention."

"I know, Phyllis, but I'm tired. We're getting ready for the Baltimore workshop. I never seem to . . ." At that moment there's another knock at the door. It's Jennifer's mom with food.

"It's so cold out. I brought you and Jennifer some warm soup. Come and have dinner in the lounge."

Before I can answer David says, "I'll watch the game here. You go and eat."

"You don't mind?" I ask. He shakes his head no. But I mind. I want him with me. He won't come to OT or PT. He's not friendly to the other patients whose support and camaraderie I can't live without.

I eat my soup and hurry back.

"Are you angry?"

"No. I just can't stand the interruptions."

"Neither can I, but I live here now."

"It's so unsatisfying. I can't get things done at home and I can't even finish a sentence here."

I'm sorry again and again and again. David packs my dirty clothes in a shopping bag and leaves.

DAVID

✳ Going home tonight I feel I should keep on going and going and going.

Instead it is nine o'clock and the phone is in my hand. I've called you. You're crying, "David, I'm sorry. You ask me so seriously about the book. How I like this part, or do I like that better or does it sound too preachy. I want to listen. I want to be critical, to praise you, to help you finish the book, but I can't think. My brain is fogged. I feel drugged. I care only about your giving to *me*. I know you are suffering. Now you stand alone and so do I. Dearest, I'm sorry."

I'm crying. I know what Phyllis is saying is true.

"Phyllis, dear, I love you. I'm sorry to be so selfish. I want you to be a part of my life, even though I know you can't be right now."

"I really don't think you need to come every night. Especially on shower night or when other people are coming."

"I think you're right," I say. "Tomorrow I won't come. Let's see how it goes."

"Okay."

"I'll call tomorrow."

"Please comfort me, David."

"I am. I love you."

"Okay, say it."

"Sleep cradled in my love."

"You too. I love you. Good night."

PHYLLIS

✳ I am in anguish. I have to call Teresa. "Teresa, how does Maureen do it? How does she go on?"

"Wait a minute, I'll let you speak to her." Maureen, Teresa's daughter, has been bedridden with multiple sclerosis for the past seven years. Unable to move and almost blind, and when she talks to me her voice is barely audible.

"I'm dumb, stupid. That's how I do it." Teresa, in the background, is reprimanding Maureen, "Maureen, you're not dumb, stop saying that." I thank Maureen, then find I have to interpret cripplese to her mother.

"Teresa, what Maureen means is that she keeps herself dumb so she can survive. But how do *you* do it, Teresa?"

"You do what you have to do. I love Maureen and I love you, too."

"You love who I used to be, not who I am and who I'll have to be. I am so much less."

"No, Phyllis, you are so much *more* now."

"How can you say that? What do you mean?"

"Listen to me, Phyllis. Now you know so much more. You have experienced things most of us will never know. *You are more.* You have always given a lot to everyone and soon you will have more to give. But you need to *take* and get well and *let others give to you*. You hate that because you know it's easier to give than to receive."

"Okay, already, go back to saying your novenas," I dismiss Teresa with an offhand crack at her religion. Her unswerving faith baffles me. But I've heard her. I know that what she has said about me being more is true in some way. But who needs this unwanted knowledge?

Crying, crying and panicked. I've still got the phone so I'll call Gwen.

"I'm driving David nuts."

"I know."

"Gwen, I want to die."

"But I want you to live. It will get better. We love you."

"I'm so ugly. I hate myself."

"So, what else is new," she laughs. "You know, when I'm driving down to see you, I think, today I'll make Phyllis feel better. I'm funny. I'm witty. I save up good stories to tell her about my family and about my friends. I bring good food. I make all these plans. Then the moment I see you I become dumb. I think, how can I make her feel better when she is so devastated? Who am I to think I can change anything? And yet I know I'll try again."

"Oh, Gwen, you do help. You and Alan make me laugh."

"Good. You will get better even if I have to will it."

"The nurse is here, Gwen, I have to go."

"What?" says Lady Di, "are you crying again?"

"Yup."

"What now?" asks Lady Di.

"How am I going to live?"

I can't. I don't want to. I'm too old, too fat. I'm not a kid who can make a new life. I've had a life and lost it. I don't want to start all over again.

Lady Di sighs royally. Pulls up a chair next to my bed and looks me in the face. "Listen, you're just afraid you can't make it. That your body won't be able to handle things. You're scared that your bowels won't get trained. You don't know how you will live through the urinary-tract infections and you *will* get them. You have to use a catheter to urinate and that exposes you to infection. It's a fact of your life now. You're scared you won't make it through the colds and respiratory infections you'll get. Your lung capacity is impaired. You can't breathe as deeply or expel phlegm as effectively as you used to and that, also, exposes you to infection. Then, too, you don't trust your body. Your body's a lot stronger than you think it is. No, you're not twenty-one and in top shape but you'll make it. So stop wimping."

She's right! I don't trust my body. That's not new. It's an old problem that is worse now. I'm afraid I'll fail gym again.

In my crowded New York City gym class, I had a friend named Jane who looked enough like me in our blue gymsuits that when my name was called she would jump up and climb the rope or clear the hurdles for me.

Tonight, tomorrow, and forever I have no stand-in, no understudy that can go on for me. Oh, Jane, where are you?

──── ✳ XV ✳ ────

PHYLLIS

✳   "No visitors tonight?"

"Where's David?"

Everyone is asking. He has become a fixture.

"David, hello, my dearest. I'm glad you didn't come, even though I miss you. No one came tonight and I'm glad."

"What did you do today?"

"Prince Valiant and I played strip tic-tac-toe in OT. The therapist had to turn a big game board for every move, because we couldn't turn in our halos. The tic-tac-toe pieces are big and we exercise our hands by lifting and placing the pieces on the square. I lost.

"I slowly pulled the zipper on my sweat suit down to reveal more and more of my brace. I reached the holes where my breasts hang out and I started to hum, "Night Train." When I got to my breasts I quickly flashed my right one and then my left one. As fast as my hands allowed I zipped up my jacket.

"The therapist screamed with surprise and laughter. Valiant was laughing, choking, and turning bright red and he says, Oh, my God, I don't believe she did that, but they're great. It was fun, my dearest.

"Jennifer and I went down to the dining room to hear some music tonight. I wriggled in the wheelchair and she got up and bounced around a little. What a couple. I wish I could dance. I hate this."

"I wish you could dance, too."

"David, I can't stand another day."

"You don't have to face another day. All you have to do is sleep cradled in my love tonight. Get your sleeping pill. Don't worry about tomorrow. I'll see you after Baltimore."

"All right my dearest, be careful and come back to me."

"Don't worry, I will."

DAVID

❋ I have finally made it to PT. I need to learn how to stand-pivot you and get you in and out of a car, so we can go to Gwen's for Thanksgiving. I stood outside of the room looking in. There are people lying on mats learning how to roll over, to breathe, to lift weightless weights in ordinary movements. I watch an eighteen-year-old learning how to sit up and push himself along on his hands. Muscle spasms are shaking his body with such violence that he falls down. Each time he rolls over, he inches his way up on his elbows, grasps his legs and pulls himself into a sitting position and starts again. I look away. I have no right to gaze so openly at people in their private hell. I dread seeing you and your struggle.

I hate this room. I feel like I don't belong. I pity these people struggling so hard to breathe, roll over, move a spoon strapped to a hand. Tasks they once did reflexively, with ease. I hate my pity, knowing how much I hate being pitied. In this emotional conflict I disguise myself as the unfeeling rock the sixties' encounter groups I attended rightly accused me of being. I present myself to you and Claire. "Let's go!" I act harried.

Having chiseled away at it for years you spot my jelly-rock act. "David, sit down on the mat."

"No, Phyllis, we have to practice stand-pivoting and getting in the car."

"Sit down and relax a minute. We have plenty of time. Anyway, look who is sharing my mat today." Valiant looks up from the two-pound weights Velcroed to his hands. "Hi, David. How are you doing? Have you come to join our crippled club?" I see the person under the injury and my prejudice and fear leave. I join the people, relieved of my rock-like isolation.

Claire demonstrates how to stand-pivot you. She is such a small person and yet she manages you with ease. You sit with your legs dangling over the mat-covered platform, knees together and feet on the floor. Claire positions your wheelchair at a right angle to you, clamps your knees between hers, reaches around your waist while you put your arms around her and lean your head over her shoulder.

"You have to make sure her head is on the opposite side of where you are going," Claire teaches. "Oh, be sure the brakes are on the wheelchair, otherwise Phyllis will end up on the floor." With a smooth, steady movement, Claire stands you up, pivots you and places you in the wheelchair. Nothing to it. A piece of cake.

I try it. It is the first time we have held each other. PT can't be all bad. I'm not smooth, but we make it into and out of the chair without dropping you. So far, so good. Now for the tricky part: getting you in and out of a car.

PT has the front end of a car available for practice. Getting in and out of the car is a stand-pivot with complications. Your halo makes your head larger and we have to be careful. We can't afford to impale you on the car. Finally we manage a few ins and outs and we are all exhausted. Especially you, my poor dear.

I wheel you out of PT. I leave, belonging now.

Thanksgiving is a beautiful sunshiny day. I drive over to Gwen and Alan's to pick up their twenty-year-old son Scott. He has volunteered to help me transfer you in and out of our car. On the way to Magee we talk about the inanities that men do until they get to know one another.

We arrive in Philadelphia just in time to be blocked off from Magee by the Thanksgiving Day parade. I explain my plight to various policemen who graciously remove the barriers and wave us through. The password of the day is *injury*.

Several nurses are in your room and I rush in, suspecting some disaster. But you are all watching the parade go by. Your window offers a wonderful view of the prefeast, pre-Christmas pageantry. An auspicious beginning for our holiday.

You are hesitant and nervous while I help you don a warm sweater and scarf. Our few previous short visits outside have warned us of your propensity to feel chilled at the drop of a breeze. The nurses, elevator people, and guards at the front door are lined up beaming like proud parents. They all wish us well and suggest we eat more than we should.

Getting you into the car proves easy. Scott stands by and makes sure your halo doesn't strike anything. The thought of banging that enormous metal protector pinned to your skull has made a nervous wreck of me. We are all elated to be on the highway heading to Gwen and Alan's.

In the middle of the highway you let out a scream, "David, David, we have to go back to Magee. I can't go. Take me back!" I jam on the brakes and pull off the highway and park.

"My God, Phyllis, what is wrong?"

"I can't go, David. I am so ashamed. I shit my pants."

Scott and I both laugh as tension drops off us. "How do you know, you shit? You can't feel it," I say with impeccable logic.

"I can tell! I can feel something," you tearfully reply.

"Here, let me check." I lean you forward and put my hand down inside your pants. I'm relieved in more ways than one when I can't locate a thing.

Scott and I laugh as I pull back to the highway. You, poor dear, are crying and saying, "What good am I? I can't even tell when I shit my pants." Scott begins to tell jokes with all sorts of scatological implications. Soon we are all laughing and Scott has endeared himself to us forever.

PHYLLIS

❋ Everything is wonderful at the Thanksgiving feast. Alan and Gwen's generosity is beyond description. In the midst of plenty, in my wheelchair, I feel so lonely and isolated I could cry. Everyone reaches into my wheelchair to touch me, to speak to me. Our children lift our grandchildren up so I can touch and feel them.

Alan holds my hands and a little drunkenly and tearfully tells me how glad he is I'm alive. I thank him for the help he has given me and curse him for saving me for my new life.

Gwen comes close and I let her know what a great friend she is. I listen to her anguish as she tells me how everyone tells her what a good friend she is, but she can't give me the one thing I want most, my life as it was.

I am so lonely. I am welded to the wheelchair. I can't reach out.

DAVID

✳ I spoke to Gwen about your constant requests for me to kill you. I need a shoulder and support. Gwen was suffering from the same problem. She said, "Everyone tells me that I'm such a good friend. What would Phyllis do without me, they want to know. What would you do, David? And the girls? And the business? I'm wonderful, they say. Where do you get the energy? they ask. I should be puffed like a peacock, my golden halo glowing for all to see. Back and forth to the hospital. Baking and cooking and buying tempting and nourishing goodies. Finding sweat suits and socks and trinkets to brighten each day. Such a good friend! I'll tell you, mister, lady, lawyer, cousins, and nurse, if I were such a good friend, I'd find an even better hospital and even better doctors. I'd be calling all over the world to find out about cold laser treatments, electric implants, and all the stuff all of you show me in newspaper clippings and magazine articles and little notes you jot down when you read about some new cure, or when you see some doctor or scientist interviewed on TV which you watch while I'm running back and forth, back and forth, back and forth. That's what I'd do. I'd make more time and find more energy and do more and make Phyllis better. But if I were a really *really* good friend—the very best friend—I'd tell her I love her and put a pillow over her head and put her and all of her really, really good very best friends out of our misery."

We both stood crying. Helplessness, pain, and anger don't leave easily. We understand and hate the end for which you plead so desperately.

The psychologist at Magee calls. "We're starting a couples' group. Would you be interested?"

"I'm champing at the bit," I answer. "I need to hear if other spouses are being hounded with suicide requests. I need some help with this."

There was a long pause before he answered, "Yes, well basically we are interested in helping couples prepare for the time when they will leave the hospital."

"Whatever you say," I lie, knowing I will present my agenda. "I think it's a great idea. When do we start?"

"Our first meeting is planned for next Tuesday at eight."

"Great, I'll be there and I'm sure Phyllis will come."

"She has already agreed and asked me to call."

I will no longer cover up your death wish and my anguish. I am going to get whatever support and help I can.

"Phyllis, I saw on the bulletin board that you won the hand-wrestling contest in PT."

"Yes, I'm the level-Seven Spinal Cord Injury Champ! I beat Wayne the Wimp."

Phyllis and I slowly file into the therapy room bringing our hesitancy and eagerness with us. The therapists Robert and Anne greet us. As people talk, each of us assesses the all-important question: What is the level of injury? Can they move their hands, arms, torso? There are four other couples in the room.

One couple, Wayne and Dorothy, are in their forties and fifties like us. Wayne has the same level of injury as Phyllis. In fact, Wayne is the man Phyllis beat in arm-wrestling to win the C7 injury championship. Phyllis has playfully dubbed him Wimpy Wayne ever since. Dorothy is soft-spoken and devoted. They have an inner peace that I envy. This is Wayne's second round in a rehab hospital.

His first trip was the result of an operation for pinched nerves in his neck. He went into the hospital walking and woke up after the operation paralyzed. He had gradually regained the ability to walk. A year later he fell and injured his spinal cord permanently. Their strong religious convictions and obvious caring for each other are solidly evident.

Fred and Sue are in their middle thirties. Fred, a roofer, was hurt in an accident at work. He fell twenty feet onto a pile of lumber. He is in an electric wheelchair which he controls by pushing a lever with his wrists. His hands are in the permanent, semiclenched position indicating that his fingers don't move. They have been at Magee for four months and are leaving in two weeks. Fred talks about the possibility of running some kind of business from their home, but he sounds very depressed. Sue is working at a job she likes, but worries about Fred being home alone all day. In hollow, falsely bright voices they talk about their hopes for the future.

Ike has asked his girl friend May to attend. May is young, blonde, attractive, and scared. Ike is still pushing to make everything normal. May seems like a leaf caught in a whirlwind. Their history together is so brief and this accident demands so much. I suspect that the stress is more than their relationship can manage.

Valiant opens by talking about diving into his brother's swimming pool, hitting the edge and floating face downward. Aleta thought he was clowning around, as usual, until it was almost too late. Luckily, she finally lifted his head up and discovered how badly he was hurt. Aleta is a very quiet and serious person. Their fears are focused on the future. How are they going to manage their new home? What kind of work could Prince do? Would his hands improve so he could go back to being a computer programmer? Aleta's issues are Valiant's issues.

Phyllis introduces herself as one of those rare over-forty women who suffer a spinal cord injury. I say that my concerns seem to be different from those of other spouses of the wounded. I want to know, "Do the other injured people here constantly talk about suicide, as Phyllis does?"

Aleta is the only one to respond. "Valiant did at first, but he doesn't say it anymore."

Phyllis asks Valiant, "But don't you still think about it?"

"Yes, I just don't talk about it."

Robert breaks the silence that follows by asking, "Aleta, how do you feel about Prince not telling you?"

"Good," Aleta answers. "I don't need to hear it."

"David, is that what you want? You want me not to talk about wanting to die?"

"Yeah," I say, "I don't need to keep hearing how you want me to kill you or you want to kill yourself. I know you are in pain. I know you are working hard as hell to learn what you have to. It's hard as hell for me coming here with you talking suicide all the time."

"Then don't come and visit," you snarl. "It will just make it easier to kill myself."

Anne takes the heat off by asking, "Wayne and Dorothy, do you have the same trouble as Phyllis and David?"

"No, we do everything we did before, it just takes longer. We go to restaurants, movies, anyplace we like. We just know that God has a reason for this." They answer in a slow, serene drawl.

"If God has a reason for putting me through so much pain, then he is mean and vindictive," retorts Phyllis in her quick New Yorkese. Then quietly, "I wish I could believe. I wish I could accept what you say. I only know this injury is too terrible to inflict on anyone."

Robert asks Fred and Sue if they have discussions about suicide. Fred says, "No, I know I have to go on. Doing the best I can." Sue gives a long dissertation on hope and God's healing power and the thankfulness for small favors. "It could have been worse, you could have been on a respirator. Be thankful."

A quiet Phyllis says, "Look, David, I didn't mean it about you not visiting. I just won't talk to you about suicide, that's all."

I feel relieved and guilty, but I accept. "Good, I can't stand to hear it anymore. I become too afraid of losing you. I thought I had no right to ask you to stop talking about suicide. I'm glad I did."

"You do, David. I don't like it, but you have that right."

I drive home that night hoping I have done the right thing in telling you to suppress your suicidal talk.

PHYLLIS

✳ After the couples' group, Nurse Di asks, "How did it go?"

"You want to hear what I learned?" and not waiting for an answer, I go on.

"Couples counseling is teaching me what my accident does for everyone else:

"It makes people grateful for small things, like walking and breathing.

"It makes people feel that their petty battles aren't important.

"It makes people know how important I am to them.

"It makes people feel vulnerable and open.

"It makes people less fearful. Lightning won't strike twice in the same place.

"It makes people humble: There, but for the grace of God, am I.

"It makes people noble. I can be their mission.

"It makes people generous. They can give me the gift of caring.

"It makes me feel like killing myself."

Di's shoe squeals on the tile as she turns and tells me, "I'll come back when you're feeling better!"

DAVID

❋ "Hello, my darling, how are you?"

"Don't ask, you don't want to hear."

"What did you think of the couples' group?"

"I think they are all crazy."

"Why do you say that? I thought it was pretty good."

"You think it's good because you are a wimp. You should have beat the shit out of me because I was so awful and mean."

"I did. Each time you were awful I kicked your foot, but you didn't feel it."

"Don't be funny. Why did you think it was good?"

"I finally got some help in talking to you about the suicide crap you are always spouting."

"So I won't talk to you anymore. I'll just do it."

"You promised not to say that. So knock it off."

"Good-bye."

"Goodnight, my dear. Sleep cradled in my love and I'll see you tomorrow."

XVI *

PHYLLIS

※ Every morning Dr. Marx and his current resident arrive when I'm being dressed. In my half-naked state this ritual takes place:

"How are you today?"

"I'm okay."

"Are you drinking enough fluids?"

"I am."

"Make sure you drink a lot. You don't want to get an infection. Remember, with a catheter you need plenty of fluids."

"I know."

"Your urine looks good, nice and clear."

"Thanks, I'm trying."

"How's your bowel program coming?"

"Okay." I feel embarrassed.

Today I break the routine and tell Dr. Marx I want to try intermittent catheterization. Maybe I can train my bladder to function on schedule and get rid of this damn urine bag appended to me.

Much to my surprise he says, "We'll try."

My permanent catheter is removed. I'm to be tapped every four hours so my bladder can learn to store urine again.

DAVID

✳ On my visit this evening Phyllis is all excited.

"David, do you notice anything new?"

I look carefully, knowing how important tests like this are. I can't spot a thing.

"Look, no leg bag. I'm trying intermittent catheterization. Every four hours I sit and tap where my bladder is. Maybe it will initiate a bladder contraction so I can pee."

"Sounds good," skeptical me says. "What does Dr. Marx say?"

"He said it's not good for me. I should keep my leg bag. It's best for women to use the leg bag. I'll get dysreflexia. But he said I can try."

"What's dysreflexia?"

"Well, if my bladder gets too full it will raise my blood pressure and because of my injury it will just keep climbing unless I pee."

"Phyllis, that sounds really dangerous, you could have a stroke."

"That's why I'm going to use a catheter every four hours. If I can tolerate it I'll try every five hours, then six. I need to do it. I can't stand carrying around my urine for all the world to gawk at."

"But, what about this dysreflexia? It can kill you."

"I just have to watch my fluid intake. If I don't drink too much, I won't have to go so much. Anyway I don't care. I can't stand this injury. I need to retain some shred of my dignity."

It's great to see you filled with fight and hope. I need to talk to someone and find out what's going on.

As if on cue, Lady Di appears.

"Dum, dee, dum, dee, dum, dee," hums Lady Di, feigning danger by mimicking the theme from *Jaws*. "Today I am going to teach you to cath Phyllis, David. Let's go."

Later, she presents me with a thick sheaf of papers on bladder control, intermittent catheterization, and dysreflexia. Late that night I read them all. I'm scared to death. You're risking a lot and I know you are determined to try.

PHYLLIS

❋   Lady Di teaches well and you, dearest, are an apt student. Your biology background helps you intellectualize what is happening. You keep things sterile, get the procedure right, and hit the mark on the first try. You and Di congratulate and pat each other on the back. Fine student, fine teacher working on a demonstration dummy. I lie there like the empty shell my body is. All I can think about is how will we ever have sex. Tubes, leg bags always in the way. I'm so ashamed.

Now I am catheterized every four hours around the clock. I proudly tell my fellow inmates, "I'm on intermittent catheterization. I have to go up and get cathed."

We sit in the halls and talk about our cathing schedules, progress we've made, what our doctors said. Sometimes we compete:

"Oh, I'm on six-hour cathing."

"I'm on eight."

"The doctor says I'll be able to try ambulating soon."

This morning I stopped to speak to Ike and his girl friend May. They tried out (euphemism for "had sex in") the family room.

"How was it?" I ask.

Ike's eyes open wide. "I can't believe you asked that."

I hear May in a little voice under his words, "Awful. So different, I had to do everything."

They think I meant sex and I guess I did. Ike still has his halo on. It must have been hell.

No rush, Phyllis.

Friends come and go from all parts of my life. This accident integrates pieces of myself that are personified by the different people who visit.

They bring stories of their dog and pony shows to entertain me. Some tell jokes, sing and dance. Others bring their empathy and listening ears. Some bring their culinary talents. All come to help.

When the weather turns nasty and people stay home, my phone rings off the hook. I am forced to get out of my room to escape the constant well-wishers and return to my real life, here in the hospital.

Out of my childhood step Joel and Tobi. Joel, my long-lost cousin whom I haven't seen for twenty years, comes with his wife Tobi. They live near Magee and visit often. I like them.

Dale of the chocolate truffles, owner of my favorite bookstore and savior of my Jodi, tells me I don't have to write about this experience if I don't want to. She says, "Maybe you just want to keep writing and doing what you did before. Write about Tough-love. Nobody says you have to become a spokesperson for quads."

Thank you, Dale, for letting me keep my old identity.

My history has come through the door with a visit from an old friend. Chloe is here. Vermont winter boots, down coat, and a rosy-red complexion.

Chloe and I have been friends for twenty years. We raised our babies in cold Vermont winters, struggled and supported each other through family deaths, husband betrayals, illness, and life's other painful tricks. On Chloe's old green sofa bed in front of the windows where the sun glanced off the snowy Vermont mountains, we shared our hopes, dreams, and ambitions. We are the kind of friends that get down-deep silly and laugh and laugh over nothing.

"Oh God, Chloe, I'm so glad to see you." We're crying and crying.

Chloe's house was always in some sort of half-finished chaos. As long as I knew Chloe and Belmont, the electrical wires that should have been attached to a fixture in the ceiling hung down, threatening to electrocute the person who came closest to them. The outside of the house was two-tone for most of its life, going from old white to old barn red or back again.

The house was heated by wood and there was never a winter when all the wood, cut from the nearby forest, was in on time. The basement, which held the large wood furnace, was so crowded with old household goods, an unused tennis table, sleds, and chairs waiting to be remodeled that the winter's supply of wood sat halfway out of the garage door. Both cars sat outside the garage plugged into electric heaters. The garage was much too cluttered to allow the cars to be parked inside so the cars were kept warm on below-zero nights by heaters. One morning the family awoke to find both cars burned to blackened shells.

"Phyllis, I love you," and she kisses my face and we cry and cry.

Mary, my friend, my support, comes to the hospital day in and day out. She pops her head in my room today looking rushed, disheveled, and missing a button from her raincoat. "I'm going to the spinal cord injury class. I'll see you later."

Tonight she is here to become smarter for me. On other nights she brings me good, healthy food which we share.

"Yech!" Mary returns. "It was awful. They don't answer any questions. All they did was show a movie. Bowel training is no fun."

I wet myself in PT and everyone congratulates me. I can pee on my own. My bladder sphincter must be working. Maybe I can learn to urinate at set times. Only Dr. Marx doesn't like it. "You'll wet yourself and you can't feel. You're skin will break down in sores."

I wet myself at lunch and the nurses don't mind catheterizing and changing me. They still think it's great.

I wet myself at two and I'm very tired. Nurse Tina tells me, "You probably have a UTI." My wonderful, spontaneous urinating may only be due to an infection irritating my bladder.

After a few days of horrendous waterworks, Dr. Marx confirms it.

"You have a UTI. We need to put your leg bag back. You need to drink a lot and take antibiotics, okay?"

"Can I try again?"

"We'll see. The Foley is the best method for you, but you're not psychologically ready to accept it."

"Leave my psyche alone. Get out."

Minutes later I am sporting a Foley. In my fevered head I become Melanie singing,

"Look what they've done to my song, Ma.

Look what they've done to my song."
Look what they did to my life, Ma.
Look what they did to my life.
Ma, you worked so hard to toilet-train me and look what happened.

DAVID

✳   My visit this evening is deadly.

"How are you, my dear?" I say in my brightest, cheeriest voice, trying to dispel your pale, motionless image.

"Awful."

"I've brought some soup from Sue Bell's Restaurant, would you like some?"

"No."

"I have some of the chicken dish you like, can I heat it in the microwave for you?"

"No, David, I just want to lie here."

"Okay, I'll sit here with you."

Your great intermittent catheterization experiment has turned into a disaster. I feel badly for you.

Later, I pack urine-soaked sweat clothes in plastic garbage bags. I have a lot of laundry to do. I feel badly for me.

It's that frantic time between Thanksgiving and Christmas. Usually we would be busy getting the presents, the tree, the dinner together, looking forward to one of our favorite holidays. But I have little patience or time for holidays this year. Besides, I always depend on you to take charge of these details. Nevertheless, this is going to be your first visit home and I want it to be a good one. I know I'll have to do the organizing I love to avoid. I call the kids and get the appropriate lists of what is needed and what is wanted.

You are in your room, sitting in your wheelchair during this visit. We carefully kiss between the halo. I notice that you are busily kneading some plastic dough to strengthen your hands. I take it as a good sign of returning energy and say so.

"I'm doing pretty well. I've started typing in OT. I'm doing exercises to strengthen my hands. Couples' group is canceled because of the cold weather—are you disappointed?"

"Yeah."

"How is the typing going? You were always such a terrible typist. Maybe this is all revenge by a former typing teacher."

Your laughing response is a joy to hear.

"No. I'm an even worse typist, but I'm enjoying trying to write again. I even have some things to show you."

You are right. Your typing is awful: run-on sentences, all in capital letters, with question marks, slashes, and numbers liberally dispersed throughout. What you have written is great fun. It's all about some elderly friends of ours about whom you have written a fantasy love triangle. My laughter encourages you to tell me other stories you want to write.

I share my Christmas list with you and we go over it together.

"David, make sure you get the kids to help. I know you can't manage everything alone."

"I know. I'm delegating as much as I can. Jodi is responsible for the tree. Heidi will get the presents for the kids and Ilene. Ilene will buy the presents for Jodi and Heidi. My job is to get Christmas dinner and I've already ordered it to be delivered by our friend Sue," I proudly announce.

"I know you're busy and the holiday comes on top of everything else. I only wish I could help."

"Your job is to stay here and learn and do what you have to do. Anyway, there is always a market for a typist. Talking about being busy, though, I have some things to tell you.

"Our Toughlove people are responding to our new phone number and address. The whole office is getting back up to speed. Gwen is putting an edition of our newsletter together. She's including an article about your accident. Hopefully, this will cut down on the phone and mail inquiries we're getting about how you are. Teresa just told me the best news of all: Our sales are up and we're starting to move out of the red at last. We should be able to start paying some salaries by next month. I hope! I hope! I even mailed out the final corrections for our book. Whew! I'm glad that's over."

"That's great, David. You guys have done a lot."

Visiting hours are over and you are exhausted. The nurses

enter to begin your evening ministrations. We say good night and kiss.

The drive home is exhilarating. A little of the old Phyllis is peaking through. I think our successful Thanksgiving outing has perked you up. I feel renewed in my effort to make a life for us.

Our evening phone call repeats the tone of the visit. Both of us are feeling hopeful.

"Phyllis, this is the first time you've taken an interest when I've talked about what I'm doing. I think that's great."

"I know. It's so hard to pay attention. It seems like another world. I try, but most of the time I can't."

"I loved your story. I hope you continue."

"I will. I enjoy the writing. I feel like I'm painting word pictures and that's exciting. I'll read you a story every time you visit, okay?"

"Good night, my dear, sleep cradled in my love."

"You sleep cradled in my love, too."

—— ❊ XVII ❊ ——

PHYLLIS

❊ I am not going to any more spinal cord injury teaching classes. They just reinforce my loss and make me wail with grief, just like they made Mary angry and helpless. I know I have lost my orgasm and I cannot imagine anything that makes up for that feeling. What good does it do to tell me that other parts of my body may become more sensitive? They reassure me, these good nurses and doctors who rush to ease my grief, that I'll enjoy the affection and not to worry, because I can satisfy you, my dearest. And then they show me with film and graphic lecture just what I'll have to do. "Watch out for the catheter. You don't want to pull it out." Won't that just turn you on, my dear? "Make sure you've emptied your bowel before intercourse. You wouldn't want to have an accident in the bed now, would you?" Isn't that appealing, my dear? And I can even get pregnant and deliver a baby vaginally. Some brave souls have done it. How do you like that one, my dear? I sit in the class crying when the instructor tells these young men that they may be able to get an erection by automatic reflex, but they won't feel a thing.

"But I'm sure you will like being able to satisfy your partner with oral sex."

" 'Hey, who the hell do you people think you are, telling me what to do with my sex?' " says one guy. 'I may be rigid' (he means no pun, just a Freudian slip), 'but to me oral sex is an unnatural act. I'll make up my own mind what to do, without your help,' he snarls. In my heart I'm saying, 'I'm glad I'm not your wife, but good for you. Speak up, say it again.' Anything being offered now is second-rate, not the real thing. How can the young single men sit there so quietly, so still? How will they explain their awkward sexuality to partners whom they have not yet dreamed of? I am embarrassed even here among my own kind. What will it be like outside?

A small woman with a partially shaved head quietly says, "How dare you make this woman cry?" And she means me. My protector has arrived. I act like I want the brutal truth but she, my alter ego, knows I don't. "If more of you had God, you wouldn't worry about sex. Be a witness," she booms out in her best preacher voice. It's obvious that her religion is a comfort and guide to her.

"Amen, sister," yells someone from the back. Some people smile. We all protest in our own ways. God again.

DAVID

✳   "David, do you love me?"

This old question of yours has a new urgency. Your voice is soft and quavering. Looking in the mirror you say to me, "How could you? Look what I'm like now." Your reflection in the mirror oozes self-hate.

I'm busy hanging up your clean clothes and waiting for the hospital microwave to be free so I can heat your dinner. "Of course, I love you. Can't you tell?" Our constant debate about love is off and running. You want kisses and caresses for reassurance. Instead, I offer tasks.

After all these years, however, I've learned. I squat next to you and give you a kiss requiring both caution and contortion. I hold your hand which quickly cramps. "What are we going to do about sex?" you whisper. I sigh and my anxiety rises. "I don't know. We'll have to wait and see."

Love and sex. Love and sex. I've never been very good at putting the two together.

I was thirteen years old when I returned home from the orphanage. World War II was in full bloom. My older brother was in the Marine Corps and on his way to battle in the Pacific. The man my mother had been living with, and just had a baby by, was drafted into the army. My mother, older sister, new baby sister, and I lived in a small, two-bedroom apartment on 145th Street in Manhattan.

My two sisters shared one bedroom, while my mother and I shared a double bed in the other. Usually my mother worked nights as a practical nurse, but there were those few occasions when we literally, but not sexually, slept together.

In my conscious mind I put no sexual connotations on this arrangement, but masturbation and sexual fantasies of girl/woman ruled my early teenage life. On those rare occasions when my mother noticed my roaring sexuality she would warn me that excessive masturbation would drive me crazy.

I didn't stop and to the best of my knowledge I'm not crazy. But I did learn a great deal about fantasy and sexual satisfaction.

My mother's puritanical exhortations and her bohemian behavior are within me. Sex means staying selfishly in fantasy. Love means doing and helping.

My early marital sex life was like masturbation, but you forced me out of my isolation. It took me time to learn about reality being better than fantasy. With your injury, I've regressed and my sex life is filled with fantasy again.

Aloud, I say, "Phyllis, dearest, I've put sex aside. I feel sexless. When you get better we'll work it out. It won't take fifteen years this time. Yes, my dearest, I love you. First, let me get your dinner together and then I'll kiss you."

Driving home I can't believe how nuts I feel.

The next afternoon, when I arrive at the hospital, it is obvious that you are having a bad day. You're sitting in your wheelchair stretched out sideways over your bed doing a weight shift. Your face is pale and tired-looking. It is impossible to get close to you, so I sit there holding your hand.

"You look exhausted, my dear, how are you?"

"I'm very tired. I just don't have any energy."

"Well, I brought some supper for us. I'll heat it up in the hospital microwave. Maybe that will perk you up," relying on the magic of food.

"I don't know. I'm not very hungry," you say, casting the evil eye over my offerings.

"I'll warm it up, anyway." I know that getting involved in doing things will help relieve my worry. I bustle about, heating food, setting the table and avoiding the reality of you.

In spite of your evil eye, the magic in the food seems to work. You perk up and become more animated as we share what now passes for intimacy. You read me a story you have written.

I leave the hospital early. I need to go to the gym. I now work out six days a week.

I lift weights to make sure I'm strong enough to lift you.

I jog four miles a day to make sure I have the physical stamina to help you.

I do neck exercises to make sure my muscles can take any sudden jarring.

I'm tired and I have to force myself to stop at the gym and not go home. The thought of two hours of exertion seems too much. But, just because I'm resisting, I work harder than usual. I will brook no shirking. I have a mission.

I am so exhausted by the time I get home that I almost give up on my nightly call. Listening to your fumbling attempts to pick up the receiver and finally hearing your whispered "hello" makes me feel good about my aching muscles. As I speak to you and hear your recital of pain and exhaustion, my own self-induced condition leaves me with nagging feelings of doubt about the tasks I have set for myself. When you finally ask me to say it to you, "Sleep cradled in my love," I'm in a full-blown downer.

I'm reaching for my old crutch, exercise, and I am determined to use it to the max. I didn't want to think this, but my aching muscles and a lack of energy followed by a short temper are forcing me to recognize that youth and vigor are no longer within reach. But when I cut through all the rationalizing, I'm just trying to prevent *me* from becoming physically helpless.

PHYLLIS

❋ Last night there was an awful thud from the room above my head, and then a Code Alert heard round the hospital. Feet running everywhere. Patients' voices in the hall anxiously asking, "What happened? Who was it? I don't know. It was on the third floor. Someone had a seizure or heart attack or died."

I knew it was the guest above my head, Inez, a country girl from North Carolina with black skin turned gray, teeth missing here and there, a gold one out of place, her hand curled around the electric wheelchair's joystick. I'd watch the dining room attendants feed her. She never ate a lot, or smiled, or spoke first, or looked at anyone, so it was not easy to approach her. No matter how many times a day I spoke with her, in the elevator, the hall, just passing by two minutes later, working on the same craft at the same table in OT, the encounter was always like the first one. But I learned about her.

"The father of my childrens shoot me nine years ago. I been like this and he been in jail evah since. Mah spasms is terrible and all the time gettin' worse. Mah doctor say they gon to help me here."

Some days Inez was tied into her chair to prevent the spasms from knocking her out of it. On other days, I noticed the foam padding between her legs pushing her knees apart so they would not knock against each other and wound her. I fear this can happen to me one day.

"Da's an operation that stops day spasms. But first I has to git real healthy," she told me. Her mamma was watching her kids at home and she "didn't have nobody up heah" who cared for her.

"Ah miss my kids," she cried.

Last night they took Inez to Jefferson Hospital. She had some sort of seizure. I hope she'll get healthy. I hope I'll stay healthy.

DAVID

✳ "I know you're not up for this, but I need to tell you some news about Toughlove. Just listen, you don't have to respond. I know you're tired. We just got a letter from a woman in New Zealand. She heard about Toughlove from a friend of hers in Hawaii. She ordered some material and is going to start a Toughlove parents' group. Isn't that exciting?"

"I don't know, David. I'm too tired."

Your nurse, Lady Di, appears.

"Is anything wrong with Phyllis?" I ask her. "She seems too tired."

"I don't think so. There are no symptoms of anything. It just happens. People have good days and bad days. This is just a bad day."

Bad days we'll live with.

I spend the rest of the evening with your head lying on my lap or sitting quietly in the chair holding hands with you.

It's difficult leaving you tonight. You are so helpless and I want to stay and protect you. Instead, I reluctantly head home. Tough-love and its successes seem insignificant.

── ✳ XVIII ✳ ──

PHYLLIS

✳   Jennifer comes in crying, breathless, sobbing.

"What happened?"

Hiccupping, sobbing, "I have to leave here."

"How come? What happened?"

"Dennis saw me stand up to weight-shift and told me I have no right to be here."

"You're crying over what that mean little turd said? He treats the nurses, his parents, everyone like dogs. He's the only one I know that almost deserves to be a quad and have acne too. Dennis is like so many of the young men who feel so helpless. They boss the nurses and treat them like servants, those lovely nurses who are my arms and legs and my body."

"I bet he's not the only one that hates me because I can walk," Jennifer moans.

"Jennifer, everyone who can't walk is jealous, even me. But if someone's walking, I'm glad it's you. You belong here. You've been hurt and are suffering like all of us. Now shut up. I have to sleep."

Falling asleep, I think of the young injured men down the hall who bolster their egos smashed by injury. Some flirt and smilingly seduce the nurses to get what they want or need. "Oh, baby, you are so beautiful, think you could stay a while and rub my back?" And then there are others like Winston.

Winston is a yellow-skinned man who was shot during a dope deal. He's twenty-one years old and has two children with one on the way. His "woman" comes every day to feed him dinner.

The bullet that injured him smashed the third cervical vertebra and severed his spinal cord. The only thing he can move is his head.

He has to have his every need met by someone else. He cannot even chase away a fly, blow his nose, wipe his face, or scratch an ear should it itch and yet he is mean as hell.

In the dining room when the nurses's aides try to feed him he hisses, "Listen, fat bitch, get that food in my mouth." Behind me, on a mat in physical therapy, he tells the therapist, "Fuck off and leave me alone, bitch, or I'll get my people on your ass." The therapist who is trying to move Winston's arm and leg joints so they won't fuse and become immovable gives up. She sits Winston up, moves him to the edge of the platform and stand-pivots him into his wheelchair. She walks away to work with someone else. Winston mumbles after her, "Bitch, bitch, bitch."

I hear through the grapevine that he sleeps with his light on and door open so he can see if anyone's coming to get him.

David looks cold, bundled up in his English sheepskin and Scotch plaid scarf. His nose is red.

He kisses me and says, "I love you."

At this moment, Myra the assistant nurse/drill sergeant, barges in. "Hey, aren't you going to the Christmas party?"

"Not if we can help it, we have couples' group tonight," David says.

"Oh, David, I forgot to tell you, couples' group has been canceled for Christmas and New Year's."

"That's good, now you've got to go, everyone worked so hard to make Christmas nice. Come on, I'll get you up," Myra bullies.

"Okay, okay." We feel obligated.

The dining room is darkened, decorated with tiny lights and tinsel. The tree is lighted. The food is good. The staff is making merry and the patients look dilapidated.

"To all of us, and especially to you, a very Merry Christmas," toasts the director.

David bends to whisper in my ear, "What are we doing here? Is this our real place now?" Against our will we have become part of this disembodied corps.

We don't want to be here, but we know we belong.

Soon I'm tired. The Christmas party has chilled us both.

DAVID

✳   Christmas Day is here and I dread it. I can't help thinking of other Christmases we have had, like the time the kids and I cut our first Christmas tree in the Vermont woods. The tree, which looked just right in the snow-covered pine grove, was too big for the house. We all laughed so hard as the kids and I cut off half of it just to fit it through the doorway. You and the kids baked loads of cookies to decorate our tree. The excitement of that Christmas morning, the kids, all the presents, and our first Christmas tree are still warm and wonderful memories.

Later Christmases were different, particularly during those unhappy years when the kids were troubled and troubling teenagers. But, still, we always seemed to pull together for this special holiday, to become a family again. Finally, there was that lovely Christmas that signaled the end of those bad times. You spent the whole year putting together old pictures of our families of origin, wedding announcements, birth certificates, recipes, family histories, and pictures right up to the present. You were letting each kid know that the family history was theirs now. We all bawled our eyes out. What a wonderful Christmas that was!

---------------- ✳

Now we have a new reality and new traditions to begin. The day is bitter cold with a steady northwest wind. Not the best for your first visit home. The kids will be getting the tree, presents, and Christmas dinner ready while I drive to the hospital to pick you up.

At the hospital your apprehension is obvious. You are surrounded by several nurses, basking in their white-covered, professional security. I, the unwelcome interloper, am here to drag you out of the nest and into the cold world. As usual, I don my mask of efficient, task-oriented maleness, smoothing out the difficulties, making our worlds safe. Pushing aside my apprehensions, I pack you in a warm sweater and your heavy Irish cape. There is nothing I can do to cover your head; the halo is too bulky and sensitive. Putting your gloves on for you is like helping a little kid. Your hands are better, but still not agile enough to make sure each finger is in the right slot. With stuffing, pushing, pulling, and packing we prepare to make the cold journey to the car. No more quick entries and escapes.

Transferring you from wheelchair to car is a carefully orchestrated chore. I make sure to clear the halo and get you comfortable (as if this state will ever be possible for you again). The wind is funneling through the garage, biting your exposed flesh and bringing tears to your eyes. I push on, determined to make everything seem natural once again.

The car heater is going full blast. I'm suffocating and you're still freezing. Getting close to home you start to cry, "Oh, David, I don't want to go home. Take me back, please."

"Phyllis, it will be all right. Don't worry. The kids have fixed everything and the grandchildren are waiting. You'll feel better once we get home."

"David, I don't want to be like this. Going home only makes it real. I don't want to live a life like this."

"It will be all right, Phyllis. Don't worry. Just enjoy the holiday. You'll see, it will work out fine," I lie, knowing I don't want either of us to have to live life like this. But it is all we've got and I don't want to face the emptiness of not having you.

I get you out of the car in a reverse of the slow, laborious process I used to get you into it. The physical exertion on my part helps keep me warm, but you, poor dear, can only sit there and take it.

This is my first attempt at getting a wheelchair into our house.

At Magee I measured the width of your wheelchair and found out that we needed at least thirty-four inches to pass through any doorway. In checking our house the doors were all thirty-six inches wide. So far, so good.

I then checked to make sure there weren't any kitchen counters or narrow passageways that I hadn't considered. There was an elevation of one and a half inches between our kitchen and living room. We had put in wooden floors with a rounded board to deal with the difference in height. You will need help to get over this obstacle, but that seemed to be our only difficulty.

My mind is racing. Did I make the right measurements? Can I wheel you over the gravel? Is there room between car and driveway for us and your chair? Despite my visions of calamity, everything fits. We burst into the warmth and tears of our family. "Merry Christmas, everyone," fills the air but not all our hearts.

We open our presents with the appropriate *oohs* and *aahs*. The grandchildren are the most fun as they go from gift to gift not knowing where to start or end. As usual, they keep looking for more even after their last gift is opened. The anticipation, pleasure, and surprise of opening brightly wrapped, carefully beribboned packages is more important than the gift. Little one-year-old Nitya is overwhelmed by it all; almost-two-year-old Ian is surrounded by a mass of torn and discarded decorations, while six-year-old Christopher only wants to ride his bicycle. For them, life goes on as usual.

"I'm freezing, David. Can't you turn up the heat?"

"I have the thermostat set as high as it will go. Here, put on this sweater, your coat, and here's a blanket." We pile up one upon the other until just a face is peering from under a mound of wraps. No matter what, the emotional warmth of the holiday and family is not enough to compensate for the drafts in our old house. Your semifunctioning nervous system can no longer keep up with the cold you once liked.

"I'm freezing. I just can't get warm."

Your hands and face are cold to my touch and your teeth are chattering. All too soon I repeat the winter dressing ritual: warm sweater, heavy cape, stuffing of fingers into gloves. Heidi warms up the car and we brave the outdoors and retreat toward the warmth and safety of the hospital. The house we had made our home has become a house again.

PHYLLIS

✳ On the way back, I pour my heart out.

"David, I only want to remember Vermont Christmases and Christmas Eves." Where black clear skies fill with bright stars and Christmas trees cut from our forest loom larger than life in the living room. To remember our small children peering down from the top of the staircase after weeks and weeks of baking and delivering packages to friends and neighbors. I want those Christmas days when our little kids opened presents and tried out toboggans and snowshoes on snow-covered roads and hills. How we walked in the cold winter sun down silent roads past snow-laden trees. And the smell of Christmas turkey greeting us at the door as we took off boots, snowsuits, and gloves wet with snow, and then how we warmed our red ears with our hands.

I want this storybook memory, not this nightmare I've just had. A trip home to a house I no longer belong in.

A house, with its empty rooms. A cold, bare place where I can't reach a cabinet, open a door, or use my brand-new stove. A house that is another symbol of how different I am.

In spite of your efforts and our children's to celebrate my homecoming, I am alone.

There is no warmth for me there, I don't know how to enter your world from my wheelchair. That house belongs to someone else's body, not mine.

You drive with tears streaming down your face.

I'm glad to get to the hospital after a pain-filled ride back. I'm relieved when you undress me and put me in bed.

Later when we talk on the phone, it's quick and easy.

"David, I forgot to look at the stairs."

"Yes. We have to sell the house," you say.

"That's right. I love you."

"I love you."

"Say it, David."

"Sleep cradled in my love."

"You too."

In the morning, Barbara, my bright, lovely morning nursing assistant, comes in to dress me.

"How was Christmas?"

"We're going to sell the house."

"Oh." And she knows how Christmas was.

XIX

PHYLLIS

※ George is an old-injury quad in an electric wheelchair.

He sits outside the lounge and looks in. He sits inside his room and looks out.

He looks like Mephistopheles. Four years ago he opened his eyes after a good night's sleep and found himself paralyzed. No rhyme or reason. The official word around here is that he lives with his sister who works all day. He stays alone and sits in his wheelchair from morning to night, although he can barely move a muscle. No one visits him at the hospital, either.

"Hello, George. How are you today?"

He gives me the inevitable answer—eyebrows up, left hand in a fist moved side to side like he's going to give me what I think of as an Italian ah fungoo sign. His wrist is all he can move. He says "So, so" through a closed mouth.

"George, how come you are never fine, or terrible, but always 'so, so'?" I finally ask him. "Don't you ever have one good day?"

"Maybe sometimes," he answers inanely.

"George, what the hell are you doing here?" I really think the hospital feels sorry for him and keeps him so he won't be lonely.

"I got insurance, so they're giving me vocational testing."

"What do they tell you you're fit for?"

"Proofreading."

That figured. I heard he was meticulous and perfectionistic, driving the nursing staff crazy about how he's sitting, the crease in his sweat pants, making sure each and every hair is in place, and giving minute instructions on how to care for him. Perhaps that's what happens to old-injury people. I can see a white-haired me screeching, "Attendant, turn me an eighth of an inch on my left hip, not a fraction more!" He constantly asks the nurses, "Did you wash my hip, my this, my that?" Even though his obsessiveness is maddening they like him and want him to have a better life. On Christmas Eve, two nurses donned sheets, made clanging noises, and went into his room to haunt and tease him. They pushed him under the hall's mistletoe and lay little pecks on his cheek. They got him to smile.

"Proofreading sounds good," I tell him.

"It's too hard."

"What did you do before?"

"I was a coin checker at a mint."

"Can't you do that anymore?"

"No. You need your hands to turn the coins."

"Can't you spell? Is that what makes proofreading hard?"

"No. I just don't want to do it."

"What do you want to do?"

"I don't know."

"Do you like it here?"

"No."

"What do you do at home?"

"Nothing. I'm alone."

"Do you like that?"

"No."

"So then why don't you kill yourself?"

"Maybe I will."

"Good thinking," I say.

Looking at him, he may need someone to help him kill himself. Maybe I'll volunteer if he asks.

"I know the perfect job for you. Be an underwear inspector in a factory. You could hold the underwear in your teeth to turn them around, and you know the little pieces of paper that fall out of the package when you just open it, and it says, 'No. Twelve inspected this product.' Everyone will know that you inspected their underwear by the bite mark in the elastic, no little paper needed. Wouldn't that be good! You could save some manufacturer lots of money." He smiles. Aren't I clever?

George and I spot Winston and his very pretty mother walking up and down the hall. "It's a boy," they tell us. Winston's mom offers the cigar he cannot hold.

DAVID

✳ "Phyllis, my dear, are you ready?" It's time for our big New Year's date! I'm excited and looking forward to spending an evening alone with you."

"I'm not sure we should go, David. Maybe we should just stay here."

"Come on, don't wimp out now. We've got reservations. We can always come back if we have to."

Reluctantly you give in and I bundle you up to go outside. Light sweater, heavy woolen sweater, scarf, and gloves engulf you. It is a quick one block down from Magee to the hotel. The biggest problem is waiting for the light to change so we can navigate the curb and cut across the street. In the few minutes it takes, your teeth are chattering. Both of us have second thoughts but I push on.

As we eat dinner, we watch people crowd into the hotel. They are here for double pleasure. Tonight they party and tomorrow they'll watch the spectacularly beautiful, creative Mummers' Day Parade and party some more.

When people see you in your halo, they quickly look away. For us, wrapped in cloaks of invisibility, their excitement is not contagious. "Look at that woman's dress, Phyllis, it's beautiful," I say, trying to lure you out of apathy.

"It's all right."

"Can you see how they've decorated the hotel? They've done a nice job," I try again.

"It's just too hard to look around."

I give up. "Come on. Let's go register and go to our room."

There is a long line of soon-to-be revelers waiting to register. I'm glad I made reservations. I park you in a nearby corner and wait on line. It's lonely being surrounded by all the playful, joyous couples.

I look over at you looking so lonely and hurt sitting by yourself. I miss the you that is my friend, my constant companion, the maker and sharer in my life. Now, with you so injured, what will our new year be like?

Finally the registration details are taken care of. We have an accessible room. We know the room is manageable. Other patients have given us the word.

"Wow, thank God, Phyllis, the worst is over."

"David, don't ever leave me stuck in a corner like that again. Everyone looks at me like I'm some freak."

Smack! Right between the eyes. I did it again, thoughtless and inconsiderate in ways I haven't even learned yet.

The room is perfect. Even the door handle is beveled for nonfunctioning hands. There is a roll-in shower, a king-sized bed, and a remote TV control. At least this much is working out.

"David, I'm in so much pain I have to lie down."

"Hold on tight, Phyllis, I have to lift you. The bed is higher than your wheelchair seat."

"Maybe we should go back, David, I'm afraid."

"Come on, wimp. We can do it." My challenge energizes you; with a little extra effort, we make it. I prop your head up with pillows, but we never find that magic position of, "I'm comfortable."

"Well, an hour and a half to go till New Year's,"
I say.

Tears are rolling down your cheeks. "I don't want to have a year like this. I can't stand it. I'm in constant pain and I hate who I am. Don't make me go on like this."

"Goddamn it, Phyllis. Can't you ever get out of your self-pity shit!"

"No, I can't. I hurt and everything reminds me of who I was and who I am now. I hate it. Take me back to the hospital. I don't want to be here. Please, David, please. Don't make me stay here."

Back at Magee, I get you into bed with the ease of familiarity.

"David, David, I'm so sorry I ruined your New Year's. I can't help it."

"I understand. I should have listened to you instead of making you do what I wanted."

"I wanted to go, too. Seeing all the other people dressed up and having fun was just too much. Please forgive me."

Together we watch the Times Square ball fall and gingerly kiss in the New Year. The hospital is quiet.

Back in the hotel room I have rented I shut out the noise of others' New Year's revelry with TV and try to sleep.

The next morning I arrive at your bedside to take you to the Four Seasons Hotel for New Year's Day brunch. You and several nurses are watching the Mummers' Day marchers getting ready in the streets below.

"How are you, David? Look at all the costumes. Aren't they beautiful?"

"I'm okay. Yeah, I saw some of the outfits as I walked over. I don't know how they do it."

"I loved thinking that you were right across the street last night instead of thirty miles away."

"Me too, especially since it made it easy to get here this morning."

Your smile is refreshing.

The weather is not too cold and our three-block walk to the Four Seasons is easy. The hotel is gorgeous with lovely flowers and plantings everywhere. The host seats us at an out-of-the-way table to protect you and others from bumping the bulky wheel-chair.

I go up to scout the goodies presented and come back to tell you what's available.

"Phyllis, you have your choice of all kinds of fresh fruit, lox, whitefish, bagels, rolls, and Danish. I don't dare describe the pastries and desserts since, as you know, you have to eat your meal before dessert."

Well, David, you know me, I have to start with dessert." And off we go. Me scouting and bringing back samples of everything for you to taste. You struggling to see and eat because the halo keeps your head tilted back just far enough so you can't see the table. I hold the food for you to see and help you lift your coffee cup.

The couple at the next table lean over and say, "Happy New Year."

We are pleased because recognition by outsiders is not too common.

"Happy New Year," we reply.

"I'm sure you'll be glad to get that contraption off your head. What happened?"

"I fell downstairs and broke my neck."

"Will you still need a wheelchair when it comes off?"

"Yes, I'm paralyzed below my arms."

"That's too bad but have a better year, this coming one."

"Yes, you too."

Back in the hospital we watch the Mummers' Parade. It seems to go on forever.

Later one of the string bands comes in to play and prance for the patients. One of their band members had broken his back and was in Magee for a while. The band was saying thanks to the hospital.

PHYLLIS

✳ Sitting outside my room, Ike, Jennifer, Valiant, and I compare New Year's notes. They went home and spent it with their families. We are all sad and happy on the New Year and wishing for much more than we have.

Ike tells us how he treated his girl friend May. I think it's a test; he doesn't. In my head I fill in the pieces of his half-told story:

"Come on, May," he said. "I don't want you feeling you just have to hang out with me. I know you like to dance. Why don't you go out with your friends? I'm all right."

May must have thought, *I want to have fun, I want to go out. I'm young.* Out loud she said, "No, really, I don't mind." Ike wished she'd say "I want to stay with you" instead of that weak, "I don't mind." The more Ike pretended it was okay and May knew he pretended, the more May felt she deserved to go. She was *his* girl, it wasn't like she was going out with another guy, until she said, "Well, if you're sure you don't mind."

"No. No, not at all. Have a good time."

She kissed him and walked through the door that had held her trapped.

When she came back Ike asked, "Who'd you dance with? Was it a guy? It's okay, you can tell me."

May pouted and lied a little, "I only danced two times with two different people."

All the while he'd hoped she hadn't danced at all. Ike turned his back to May and asked, "Did you have a good time?"

"It was okay. What did you do?"—hoping to change the direction of the talk.

How he must have wished she'd fight him to stay!

How she must have wished it was all right to go!

Things are not good.

I'm glad David fights me.

Winston's Mom has brought the baby for him to see, even though he won't be able to touch him. He is so proud as he says, "This here's my son. My third son, Malcolm." I imagine him adding, "Real men make sons. Ain't I a real man." His mother shows everyone the baby she carries in her arms. It is a pretty, butter-colored child. "The baby is beautiful," I say and feel its soft, soft cheek. Winston beams like he's really accomplished something.

──── ✳ XX ✳ ────

DAVID

✳   The temperature is hovering near the twenty-degree mark and yesterday's sleet has become today's ice-slick road. I'm tempted not to go to the hospital but I haven't seen you for a few days. Our daily phone calls are not enough, particularly the last one of each day. You are alone in your room, the day's events have exhausted you, yet sleep eludes you. Our phone conversations at this time are filled with your expressions of doubt, fear, and sadness. Our ending of "sleep cradled in my love" offers me the relief of immediate escape. At least when I visit, I see other realities. Your gregariousness with other people gets you animated and involved. You lose your injured self and become filled with life again. I need these moments to help me through. I need to see your joy, hear some laughter, share in your moments of liveliness, brief as they are now, to help me slog through my own doubt, fear, and sadness.

While driving, I allow my thoughts to ramble. As usual, snow and ice remind me of Vermont. Like the time we left New York City in a driving rain storm and arrived in Vermont with rain still falling. The minute we started to drive up the hill to our house, everything changed. The slight elevation caused enough of a temperature change to turn everything into glare ice. The car quickly stopped its forward motion and began sliding backward down the hill. I had no control; we slid to the side of the road and came to rest in a ditch. We only had a mile to go and decided to hoof it. Wrong again. The road and fields were coated with smooth, hard ice and we couldn't even stand up because of the slope of the hill. Luckily, the town plow truck came by spreading a magic mixture of salt and sand. Our car needed to be towed out of the ditch, so Mr. Ghostland, driver of the plow truck, gave us a ride home. I stood on the running board with you and Ilene, while Heidi and Jodi rode in the truck. Mr. Ghostland kept up a running commentary all the way up the hill to the house, where he came in for a drink. He entertained us with stories filled with dry Vermont humor about newcomers and Vermont winters.

Déjà vu. I hit an icy spot and the car takes on a life of its own. I slide over and brush against the side rail which propels me into the opposite traffic lane. Fear grips my heart and a vision of the two of us in wheelchairs flashes before me. Then quickly, as the oncoming car is heading toward me, I get onto a non-icy spot. My car belongs to me again and I get back on my side of the road just in time to avoid oncoming traffic. Enough daydreaming. I take the remainder of the ride to the rehab with caution. Phyllis's injury fills me with reminders of my own fragility. I feel great relief walking through the doors of Magee. I know I won't share my misadventure with you.

"How are you, my dear?" I say, looking closely for the vital signs.

"I missed you, David, I'm so glad you're here. I thought the weather would keep you away."

"Come on, Phyllis. You know that after living in Vermont, a little snow and ice won't stop me. Tell me, what's new?"

"Do you remember George, the quad who always sits outside and looks in?"

"Yeah, what about him?"

"George was sent to the psychiatric unit at Hahnemann. I didn't even realize he'd left. We forgot each other so quickly. But, the big news is Valiant got his halo off today and I have an appointment for an x ray in two days. If the bones are set, they'll take my halo off."

"Oh, how wonderful! I've been waiting and waiting for this day."

"Not me," you whisper.

"How come? Do you want to stay in that damned halo?"

"No, but taking it off means everything is real. I'm a quad and I'll always be a quad. I'll never stand. I'll never walk. Christopher, Ian, and little Nitya will only know me as a cripple in a wheelchair. At least with the halo, I could pretend it wasn't real."

The wind goes out of my sails, so I just hold you in the awkward way we have developed.

"Oops! sorry you guys," Prince Valiant says as he wheels into your room. "Am I interrupting anything?"

We both say, "No," glad for the interruption. Prince Valiant is there with Aleta and he is beaming.

"I got my halo off today. Boy! talk about getting out of prison."

He has a hard, foam-rubber collar around his neck with small bandages on his forehead, marking where the halo had been screwed against his skull. It's great to see him freed from that horrendous device.

Phyllis jumps into action. "How was it? Did it hurt? Is your neck stiff?"

"There was nothing to it. A piece of cake. You go into a room and in five minutes it's all over. You know what? My halo weighed eleven pounds."

"How about your neck? Can you move it?" Phyllis repeats.

Prince Valiant demonstrates how he can move it a little past the restriction of his collar. "To tell you the truth, my neck feels weak and funny. I'm really afraid to move it too much. It'll take a couple of weeks for my neck muscles to get strong and the vertebrae to loosen up."

"How was it for you, Aleta?" I ask.

"I was nervous. I still am. I'm afraid the slightest jolt or movement will make things worse and then it's back into the halo. But it's so great to see Valiant's whole face and be able to kiss him without fear of losing an eye." We all laugh and the tension is gone.

"Come on. Let's go eat. I want to show my new face to

everybody." Valiant leads the parade to the dining room. Gregarious Phyllis appears and she gets out of herself and into the people. It's fun basking in the curiosity and interest of the yet-to-be-freed patients, stimulated by the relief Prince Valiant and Aleta are expressing.

After a cautious drive home, I call the hospital for our final conversation of the day.

"Oh, David. I'm so afraid. What if I get the halo off and nothing changes? What if I'm still so tired and in pain all the time?"

"Phyllis, you know getting your halo off is just one step. You'll have better balance without all that weight on your head. You'll be able to start transferring yourself to and from your bed and we can actually lie next to each other."

"Yes, that will be nice. David, will you go with me when I get the halo off?"

"My God! Phyllis, how could you even think I wouldn't? Of course, I'll be there."

"That's good. I'm tired tonight. I hope I can fall asleep quickly," you sigh.

"Good night, my dear. Sleep cradled in my love."

"Good night, David. You sleep cradled in my love."

PHYLLIS

✳ Today, in the elevator, a nurse who is taking Winston to physical therapy tells him how lovely his baby is. Winston, who has returned to normal snarls, "Better than yours, you fat bitch."

A disgusted nurse says, "You are nasty, nasty." As the elevator door opens I lean toward him and whisper, "I feel sorry for you. You're so helpless and no one likes you."

"Get out of my face," I hear him say as I move down the hall under my own power.

All the nurses are complaining about the family down the hall. They are noisy, whiny, they don't do what's asked. They won't leave when visiting hours are over. The grandchildren of the injured woman are running wild and the family fights about who's going out for dinner, who's watching the kids. They create havoc. Everyone complains. Finally, David goes to the room, calls her son and daughter out, and tells them they're disturbing everyone. They cringe and cool it from then on.

Lucille, the patient, is being treated for, of course, bedsores. She's embarrassed to go to OT and PT on the cart, so she looks away a lot. She has her own private-duty aides who come to the hospital to care for her.

She was in an accident that, she assures me, "paid off well," a hard injury to afford, "so we got money at least."

Her room is cluttered with bags from Kentucky Fried Chicken, McDonald's, and Wendy's. I think a party went on here. She is a C5, 275-pound quad whose hands are useless but her nails are polished and manicured. That night I talk with her and she reassures me that I'll get used to it. "It's not so bad being taken care of. I just fired my evening attendant because she didn't do my hair nice."

"Lucille, I don't want to get used to this."

"Give yourself a chance, you'll manage, darlin'. It's been five years and at first I wanted to die, but now I get enjoyment from my livin', my kids, my grandchildren."

And all I can think is, you're back in the hospital.

"Wait till you see me when I'm dolled up. I look pretty good. I'll show you in a few days. I'm goin' home."

This afternoon Winston is in front of the nurses' station yelling as loud as he can. "I'm getting outa' here. Don't you know who I am? Where the hell is the nurse? I ain't goin' to that f-ing therapy. The doctor can kiss my black ass."

I ask Lady Di, "What's wrong with him?"

"His baby's mother got shot to death today." She shakes her head sadly. "He's insisting on going home and I guess he's next. God, what a waste."

On Saturday, Lucille's attendant knocks on the door and wheels her in wearing a gray pantsuit, make-up fine, hair coiffed, and around her shoulders and pulled down under her tush is a beautiful black mink coat. She says, "Now you know, chile, that if it weren't for this accident, I wouldn't of had me a fine black diamond mink coat. Bye, honey."

Jennifer comes to talk, while we savor the healthy macrobiotic food Jodi has brought me.

"Phyllis, I feel so guilty saying this. I can't stand to be around my mom. She's always telling me how I should feel. She just wants this to be over; she wants me to be all better. I can't exercise hard enough for her. If she ranges my arms she always hurts me. I can't tell her I don't want her to come so often. She's always so hurt. I hate to hurt her, but she's driving me crazy." Jennifer stands up, her version of the weight shift.

Jennifer's mother cannot listen to her grief. It's too painful to witness her child's suffering. She rushes to cover her own anxiety with superficial hope. "It will be all right. You'll work harder. Stop crying and think positive." I hear her voice in my head. The next phrase I expect is, "Cheer up, cheer up; every cloud has a silver lining." I turn off her mother's voice.

Jennifer's father is no protection. He cannot talk or listen now because he never has.

The half-crazed parents of youngsters so badly maimed come every day. No matter how hard they work, how tired they feel, or whether their kids want them or not, they are here. All of us are thrown back on the healing magic the presence of a loved one brings.

"Jennifer, kiddo, I think we're all crazy. Your mom hopes she can will you better, I guess."

Jennifer, who's in her whining mode, whines. "She makes me feel like I'm malingering. How am I going to live at home? I know I have to; who else will take care of me?"

Aha, I think, therein lies the rub.

"Jennifer, you play right into your mother."

"How?" she sobs.

"You tell her every complaint and pain you have. Here's what you sound like. Mom says, 'How are you?' and you whine, 'Mamma, the nurse made me get up for PT when I didn't have to; the brace is killing me; it will never come off; I think my little finger stopped moving today and no one is paying attention.' What alternative does your mother have, then, but to be your cheerful, optimistic self, your not-helpless being?"

"I'll fix it; I'll talk to them; cheer up," she replies.

"Stop playing, Jennifer!" She looks hard at me and then we both laugh.

Jennifer asks, "What have you got to eat?"

"Graham crackers."

We drown our sorrows in food.

XXI

DAVID

✳ "Hi, Phyllis. How are you, my dear?"

"I'm okay."

I lean down and kiss you and your returning kiss would chill an Eskimo.

"Are you ready for couples' group? It seems like such a long time since we've gone."

"I don't want to go."

"You're going. I'll wheel you. You can't stop me from making you go."

"Don't you dare. That's mean," you say, bursting into tears.

"Look, if you don't go, I'm going anyway."

I want Phyllis to come with me but I know how stubborn she can be. I want to be with other people who are going through the same thing I am. I talk to Gwen and Teresa but it's not the same. They sympathize. They empathize. They help me get the time to visit you and keep Toughlove afloat. The camaraderie of sharing similar pain and struggle creates a bond that goes beyond what others can offer. I see it and feel it when Phyllis meets other patients. They try to include me but often their mutual experiences and in-common language leaves me out. At least in couples' group I am one of them.

"Phyllis, I'm going," I say walking out the door.

"Wait for me," I barely hear.

Relief floods over me. I didn't want to go to group by myself.

Only Aleta and Valiant are with us tonight. Wayne and Dorothy went out and Fred and Sue have gone home.

Valiant starts off, "We went to visit the house we bought one week before my accident. It's weird to see this place we were looking forward to from my new disadvantage point. The house is two floors, and the bedroom and only bathroom I can get into are on the second floor." Both Valiant and Aleta look awful. "I can probably slide down the stairs but then how do I get in and out of the chair? The only solution is a seat I can transfer into that goes up and down the stairs electrically. We'll need a wheelchair on every floor."

Aleta bursts out crying, "I don't want a wheelchair on every floor." Phyllis reaches over and takes Aleta's hand. They both sit there hugging and crying. I reach over and put my arm around Valiant, who sits with his shoulders sagging.

After a period of silence, Anne, the therapist, asks, "What have you and Phyllis decided to do about your house, David?"

"I don't know. After Christmas we both wanted to sell it but the physical and occupational therapy people have said we should wait. They will come out and look the house over and tell us what they think. I don't know what to do. I don't even know how to think about it."

"How could we possibly keep the house, David? I can't use anything in it. I don't know if I can live there. It only reminds me of who I was."

"I know but I'm worried about money. We can lose our whole investment in selling a half-finished house. We don't have a lot of equity anyway. How will we be able to get another house?"

"We're in the same boat," Aleta says. "Our house is in a way-out place and we'll probably have to spend money we don't have. I was happy when we bought the house but now I feel like this is another loss we have to live with."

This injury forces compromises in everything. Phyllis and I

decide to ask the physical therapy and occupational therapy people to look at our house.

After couples' group, Valiant, Aleta, Phyllis, and I sit quietly talking. It's not the words that are important, it's the huddling against the fear and insecurity of the world outside the hospital.

PHYLLIS

✳ Jennifer's physical therapist took her out for a walk and lunch. She came back, staggered into my room, and announced loud and clear, "I'm ready to go home! Wednesday I'm leaving!" And, in a small voice, she whispered, "I'm scared. How will I manage the brace . . . my mother?"

"You'll manage. Stop ruining the good news of getting out," I command.

Surprisingly, she stops and tells me she'll have some nursing at home—her mother works all day—and when she feels stronger, she's going to look into taking some courses at the community college. Now she's off to call her mom without whining and tell her the good news. Late at night, Jennifer comes to the head of my bed and whispers that she's still scared. I tell her how much I'll miss her. Strange how much easier a relationship is between an older and younger woman when they are not mother and daughter.

On Wednesday, Jennifer comes to say good-bye. We cry. Jennifer promises to visit me when she comes to outpatient care. Do well, dear Jennifer.

Next door to me is a prone-cart victim. I saw him in OT. He is half alive and not very alert. Rumor has it he is an old soldier, a former major suffering from bedsores. Big smelly holes in his body.

I see the nurses, in sterile garb, trek in and out of his room to treat him. His tall, thin, well-dressed, red-coated, bangle-braceleted, cigarette-smoking, perhaps whiskey-drinking, husky-voiced wife is occasionally in the hall. I only hear him and never see him.

All night he yells, "Oh, God, Jesus, help me!" At first, I am empathetic and sorry for the poor man. But he carries on night after night and I'm getting tired. "Can't you sedate him?" "We do, but . . ." is the answer.

One night I'm in the hall and he starts, "Oh God, Jesus, Oh God, Oh Jesus, help me!" I stop outside his room and ask him what he wants. "I'm cold," he bellows.

"So, why don't you call a nurse to bring you a blanket instead of wasting God's time?"

He laughs. Soon he's calling for God's attention again.

One night David stops outside his room and tells him, "This is God and go to bed." He laughs.

Another night I yell, "This is God. I command you to sleep." And he's quiet for a while.

On Wednesday morning last week they took him to a nursing home.

The empty room is soon filled by a very interesting client. Two policemen march in a tall, dark-skinned man in his early twenties. He's wearing a halo on his head but he can walk. The injury to his spinal cord is incomplete and the halo is holding the vertebrae in place until the bones heal.

"What's going on next door?" I ask my hospital pipeline, Lady Di.

"Charles, the patient next door, was in a high-speed chase. The car he was in crashed into a storefront and he injured his neck."

"Why were the cops chasing him?"

"Well, they think he robbed a bank. He'll be all right, though."

"An alleged bank robber will walk again and probably allegedly rob again. I can't tell you how thrilled I am."

Lady Di gives me a look of disgust and leaves. She is a professional; a patient is a patient to her.

The next day, Charles, the walking quad, comes to spinal cord group. His two police escorts sit outside. Introducing himself he says, "My name is Charles and I'm grateful to God that I can walk. Praise the Lord. I'm so grateful that I'll go to church with my mom every week. I'll serve God." It seems to me that he leaves out, "Especially when I see all you suckers in those wheelchairs." Everyone looks at each other and smirks.

Our psychologist ignores him and goes on, "Some of you are going home or have been home already. Can we talk about the best and worst parts of being home?" Charles quickly gets into the act, oblivious to everyone else. "I haven't been home yet, but when I get there I'm sure it will be wonderful," and he adds, "Praise the Lord."

I've had it. "Listen, Charles," and I'm looking him straight in the eye, "you better cool it," and I look at every smirking face, "we all know who you are." He's quiet.

After group, the guys who used to be "smooth corner boys" come up to me and say, "You don't take no shit, mamma."

"You got balls, mamma."

Later in physical therapy these guys are trying to teach me "wheelies."

✳ XXII ✳

PHYLLIS

✳ The halo's coming off and everyone is happy but me. I know that when it's off I still won't be able to walk. It's just another landmark of how permanent my situation really is.

Now strangers in restaurants can see that I am being treated for what ails me. The waiters, clerks, sales people see me on my outing and think, "Oh, she'll be all right when her head is out of jail." Later they'll think thoughts like, "Isn't it wonderful how she gets around, and her husband is so good!" Later they'll think, "Poor man, to be so burdened, what a pain." So tomorrow my halo comes off. I am getting better and better, but not in every way.

DAVID

✳ It's off-with-your-halo day and the weather is cooperating, the roads are clear and dry. I'm looking forward to the removal of your halo. When I express my enthusiasm about getting the halo off I'm concerned about how you will respond. You shoot me down with, "It just proves I won't be any different than I am now," and I say, "Phyllis, you have that knack for identifying flies in the ointment. How come you never recognize the ointment?"

The people at the rehab hospital are in the middle of their morning routine when I arrive. Self-driven, motor-driven, and nurse-propelled wheelchairs are migrating toward the elevators bearing sacrifices for the gods of physical therapy. Prone carts with patients whose bedsores have taken sole possession of their buttocks, hips, knees, or ankles have formed their own parade. These prone-cart patients have only head and arms visible while the rest of them is covered by sheets suspended on a frame over their body. Seemingly disembodied heads and arms propel themselves down the hallway. They form into various clusters of talking heads.

Barbara, your morning nurse, is helping you get ready. The two of you are enjoying an exchange of hospital gossip. Your relationship is warm and friendly. I feel I'm in an alien world so I quickly get into the numerous tasks of preparing for your trip to Jefferson. Sweaters, scarfs, gloves, an extra sweat suit, a check with the nurses' station on arrangements for the ambulance. Finally, we are on our way for a six-block ambulance ride and it isn't until we are on the crowded street outside Jefferson Hospital that we are alone.

The elevators at Jefferson are always crowded. And even though people are aware of our wheelchaired presence they make no room. Eyes averted, faces guilty, they push in and look relieved when the closing elevator door excludes us. Our strategy is to watch the lights showing a descending elevator, park in front of it, and wait. Valuable techniques we are learning to help us live in the world of "walkies."

When we see the surgeon your x ray looks good and he admires his handiwork.

"Yes, here is where I wired the vertebrae together. Here, you can see it clearly in this shot. Now this is where the bone graft is. See these shadows? It has healed nicely. You're ready to get the halo off now. You'll wear a hard collar for a while until your neck strengthens."

"Doctor, why did you bother? I don't want this life."

"Phyllis, when I first started working with spinal cord injuries, I thought everyone should go on with their life. A young man with a very high injury made me realize the choice of life or death belonged to him. When he killed himself, I was devastated. I had done all I could to help him and it wasn't enough. I think about him often. I've seen a lot of injuries. I don't think I would want to live with an injury like his, but you have more going for you than most."

"Yeah, a crippled, painful body. Fingers that get cramped and stuck. How can I write?"

Angry now, he says, "Yes, you have that. But you also have a career you can return to. You know, Phyllis, some people see a pony and think about riding. Others see a pony and think about all the manure they have to clean up. You are sensitive and smart. You have a lot to give to others. Believe me, you'll find ways to do what you want. Give yourself time. You are still just learning how to live again."

Underneath his white-coated exterior lives a man.

The technician, a tall, slender black man, arrives to remove your halo.

"Aren't you one of those people who put this on me?" you ask. I'm flabbergasted that you could remember anyone at that time. At first, he's not sure. "Oh, yeah, now I remember. We had a hard time fitting you. They don't make halos for women and it took us a while. By the way, do you want to take the halo home with you?"

"What!" we both exclaim, "why should we want it?"

"Well, some people take them home for flowerpots or something."

"Yecch! We never want to see it again."

"You never know what people want, so I'd rather ask."

In ten minutes, you're free and we are on our way. It is so good to be able to see your face again. Your long hair is a little ragged at the spots where they shaved away your hair so the halo screws could attach to your skull. I carefully hold your head in my hands and give you our first real kiss in a long time.

You are busy seeing how much you can move your head within the confines of your hard collar. I'm busy telling you to take it slow. A new switch. You the physically daring one, while I am the coward.

Back at Magee, we rush around to show everyone your new

look. Everyone is pleased for you and with you. Prince Valiant rolls up and the two of you awkwardly embrace and kiss. Ike is so pleased he pretends to meet you for the first time. Soon exhaustion takes over and I put you to bed with special care. Your neck is more fragile with the halo off because of the atrophy of your neck muscles. God forbid any jarring should happen now. But lying in bed next to you with the soft warmth of your cheek on mine feels wonderful.

PHYLLIS

✳ Now my halo is off, I can clean my full face for the first time in three months. So what! I'm exhausted. People are congratulating me and telling me how wonderful I look. Actually, I'm tired and feel sick and weak. My neck hurts and my shoulders are emaciated. This is punishment.

There are a lot of firsts now.

1. Nurses tying my bra straps together to stop the straps from falling off my atrophied shoulder muscles, the way mothers tie with small ribbons the straps of their little girls' bathing suits.

2. I see how far my breasts have collapsed onto the muscleless roll under them.

3. I see and feel my own vagina again. I find I have good feelings there.

4. I try to catheterize myself and I see that I don't yet have the hand strength to do it.

5. I know I can put on my own makeup and tweeze the hair on my face—what a relief!

6. The best thing is that when you visit me we can lie next to each other in bed. I can feel and hold you.

Heidi brings Christopher to see me without my halo.

"Grandma, I'm so glad it's out of your head." Christopher is truly relieved, another bonus.

Hal calls to congratulate me on my halo's demise. I have asked him to visit and talk to me of his faith.

Tonight Hal comes and I ask him, "How will I be able to live like this?"

"I find the Torah's teaching a way for me to be; it gives

meaning to life," Hal tells me. "Judaism gives ethics, a family life; it values community."

"I thought psychological perceptions were a way to live my life or to understand it, Hal. But I was wrong, psychology is empty."

Hal shakes his Freudian orthodox head and agrees with me.

"But, I don't believe in God."

As Hal responds, I think about all the ways I hear God talked about: *I know I don't talk to you often, God, but . . . Please, dear God, let me . . . Please, dear God, if you only . . . Oh, my God! Oh, my God in Heaven! God Almighty! God damn! God bless! Good God! God help me! God help him! Only God knows! God heals. Thank God! There but for the grace of God . . . God forbid! God love you! God strike him dead!*

I say to Hal, "As a child I thought there might be a God but now I do not feel God in my life for good or bad, for punishment or comfort. I do not understand God concepts although I truly do want comfort, hope, and reassurance. But in my childhood vision, I still try to summon God for help, for bargains. No answer comes that the child in me can comprehend."

"Don't worry," Hal says and I fantasize him tapping his fingers together tent-style, head covered by a prayer shawl, bending forward and back, forward and back.

He says, "You'll see Brucker."

People are still telling me, "There must be a reason for this accident, God must have a plan." They theorize that I must have some great mission to do or lesson to learn. "Past karma," Jodi offers. I'd like to hit them all in the head. If they only knew that I've just remembered an experience I had in San Diego that proves God is Fred Astaire.

"Hello, may I speak with Mrs. York?" the perky little voice sparkling with wholesomeness on the other end of the line chants.

"This is she," I reluctantly admit.

"My name is Jane and I'm calling to welcome you into the neighborhood."

I already know this is not a friendly neighbor calling on this bright, sunny Dan Diego morning. I am about to hear the second sales pitch of the day and the eighty-seventh sales pitch in three months. Singer Sewing Machine, Electrolux Vacuum Cleaner, Avon, Tupperware, and even good old Fuller Brush have recognized our lovely presence in our garden-type apartment and most transient of places. We are surrounded by a boulevard of fast-food joints where my rural-Vermont children were acclimating to the pop-food culture. Dining on McDonald's, Taco Bell, Mr. Pie Man, Baskin-Robbins, and Arby's Roast Beef, and they were already having trouble in school.

Through my haze of culture shock I heard my new friend, Jane the pitchwoman, say "Fred Astaire Dance Studios wants you to have five free lessons."

Without a thought I say, "Gee, I'd like to take you up on your wonderful offer, but I have no legs."

Jane is silent and then an awesome shriek and "Oh, my God, it's finally happened." I can hear the phone crashing down at the other end. I go back to housecleaning.

Valentine's Day has arrived. This is the first time I have the energy and desire to get involved in a family celebration since the accident. David and I go across the street and buy little doggies, a teddy with a pasted-on heart, a box of heart-shaped candy and Valentine cards for our children and grandchildren.

The shopping is difficult. No more moving quickly, looking behind counters or in out-of-the-way corners. David pushes me at his own pace and I have to tell him to speed up or slow down. He takes things off of shelves that are too high for me to reach. In spite of all the inconvenience I still like shopping.

At Magee we celebrate our love.

"I have no words to express my love of you. I'm overwhelmed by your loyalty, devotion, and caring. I adore and admire you."

"I love you, my dearest," you say and we hold each other as close as possible in this narrow bed of mine. I think to myself, What kind of lover will I be to you, my dearest sweetheart?

This night I hear through the grapevine that Ike and May are no more except for a long rambling, "I'm okay, it's all right" phone call. It's over.

Quad Lloyd, in therapy, finally asks the questions every young person is thinking.

"Who's going to love me enough to want to get involved with my physical care?"

How will I know love from pity?

Will I attract only misfits?

Will I ever make it with anyone?

"I don't know what to say. I'm so sad." He is very quiet.

In comforting Lloyd some men tell bold-faced lies. "Don't worry, man. I let them know I'm a great lover, try me." A twenty-two-year-old, shot in the back in a street fight, says, "You can do anything, man."

Some men lie evasively. "When I'm with her, you'd be surprised at what I can do," says a twelve-year veteran of spinal cord injury. Both men are bullshit artists. Most of us in the group are quiet.

Our psychologist says, "Poeple will want you for yourself. You are more than your injury."

I would hate to be young, in a wheelchair, trying to find and be a lover.

DAVID

❋ "David, did you remember that we have couples' group tonight?"

"Yeah, Phyllis. But you surprise me. How come you are talking about group instead of me? You're not planning to go, are you?"

"Valiant has invited a friend of his from work who was hurt two years ago. His wife is coming also."

"Sounds good. I'll warm up dinner in the microwave and then we'll go."

Valiant, Aleta, their friend Bob, Bob's wife Helen, Phyllis and I are the only people in the couples' group besides Anne, the therapist. After introductions Bob begins talking.

"I was cleaning the outside of the windows on the second story of our house when I fell over backward and injured my spinal cord. Technically, I'm a para but I can walk with crutches now. It took me a year and two trips into Magee for rehab to learn how."

"The first time Bob came home," Helen adds, "he was in a

wheelchair. I went to work every day and Bob took care of himself. I was afraid to leave him at first but he managed very well."

The thought of Phyllis or Valiant being left alone all day seems out of the question. Valiant is getting some movement in his legs but minimal movement in his hands—how would he manage? Phyllis's hands are getting better but she hasn't the strength or energy to manage very well in the hospital—how would she do at home?

Bob and Helen go on about his gradual recovery, getting to physical therapy and eventually back to work. Their struggle sounds difficult, but their cool, almost didactic presentation puts me off. One thing is clear though: All cripples are not created equal.

On the way back to our rooms Valiant comments, "I used to feel sorry for Bob at work, seeing him pull himself around on crutches. Now, I envy him. I can't see how I'll be able to get back to work. The place isn't built to accommodate wheelchairs and my hands can't work computer keys."

Aleta almost whispers, "I should have asked Helen how she got over feeling super responsible and cheated." Valiant looks away.

"I guess for me, I just stuff my feelings and do what has to be done," I tell her.

Phyllis quietly asks, "Do you feel cheated, David?"

"Yes, my dear, I feel *we've* been cheated."

Valiant says, "I don't think we need the group; there are only the four of us and we talk better without it."

We all agree and Phyllis will tell Anne tomorrow about our decision.

PHYLLIS

❋   "Anne, we all decided that we don't want the couples' group."

"How come?"

"It's only the four of us and we seem able to talk more intimately without the structure. Like last night, bringing in a couple from the outside was distracting to the closeness we've developed. The real point is, we talk better without them."

"Don't you think it gave you food for thought?"

"That's a diet I think I can go without."

Anne laughs and says, "Okay, it's your decision."

In occupational therapy, patients are working at ceramics, woodworking, typing, and playing games, all designed to strengthen arms, hands, or stroke-damaged brains. I see Charles, our prisoner quad, working at sanding a very large wooden key to hang real keys on. I can't resist wheeling up to him and saying, "That key won't open your prison cell."

"I'm not going to jail. I didn't do it."

"Then how come you were in the car?"

"Well, I was hitching a ride on Henry Avenue and this white dude picks me up and when we get in town he says he needs to stop at the bank. I'm just sitting in the car when he comes out of the bank running, jumps in the car, and drives off like a madman. All I can hear are the sirens of the police cars chasing us and I'm scared to death. This dude crashes the car and the last thing I see before I pass out is him running down the street. I'm innocent. I'll be out on bail soon."

"Then how come they found you in the driver's seat?"

"I don't know. I must have fallen over when we crashed."

"Right, Charles." And I wheel away.

✳ XXIII ✳

DAVID

✳ "Hello, my dear, how are you?" As usual, I scrutinize your face, your body position, how you move your hands. Today everything looks good.

You are not pale as a ghost or leaning on the bed exhausted. Instead you are busy kneading putty for hand strength. I find it still strange to see your entire face now that it's free of the halo. The indented scars just above your eyebrows are fading reminders. You have piled your hair on top of your head, arranged with special care. Your makeup has been studiously applied.

"Happy anniversary," I say, handing you twenty-eight different colored roses. One for each year of our marriage.

"Oh, David, they're magnificent. Where did you get them?"

"You know, Phyllis, each year of our marriage has been so

unique and different, so I searched the whole world and found each rose in a different place." Your laughter reminds me of long ago.

"Hurry, David, get them in water so they'll last as long as possible." I get the vase, cut the stems, add the florist's fountain-of-youth powder, water, and roses. As usual your aesthetic eye is offended by my haphazard setting. You busily rearrange the roses. Your less-than-perfect hand and finger coordination doesn't interfere with your pleasure. Visual and olfactory beauty fill the room.

We're off to the Four Seasons Hotel to spend the day. Our insurance won't allow you to be out overnight, so, like Cinderella, we must return by midnight. We've packed our emergency-just-in-case-satchel containing Chuxs, which are large, disposable pads to protect skin, clothes, or bedding in case of an uncooperative bowel or bladder, an extra leg bag in case of sudden punctures, alcohol swabs to clean up urine, and pills for bowel and stomach problems. We are all prepared and even the weather is cooperating. It's one of those deceptively warm February days, just nice enough to raise hopes for any early spring. The Four Seasons is beautiful and gracious. Their regular rooms can't accommodate wheelchairs very well so they offer us a suite at the same price. We settle into the lap of luxury and top it off with dinner in our room.

"David, let's get in bed. I want to lie with your arms around me. I need to be close." Without your halo weighing you down everything is much easier. Standing and pivoting you from place to place is almost becoming routine.

"David, I miss this the most. I'm so lonely."

"Me, too. It seems so long ago since I held you."

"David, what should we do about sex? Should we try it?" you whisper in a voice filled with apprehension.

I'm not ready. What should I say? I feel like a kid getting laid for the first time. "Yeah, let's try it, Phyllis, but I don't know exactly what to do."

"Me either, but let's try." I'm fumbling to remove your pants. I'm frightened about pulling out your catheter.

"Oh! My God! David, David, I have to shit. Please do something."

"Come on, Phyllis. It's just like Thanksgiving. Just relax."

"No, no, I'm going to shit. Oh, what can I do?"

"Okay, okay, don't worry, we've got a bunch of Chuxs here. I'll put some under you." I put you on your side and stick a bunch of Chuxs under you. Just in time.

"I'm so embarrassed. Oh God, just let me die. I can't go on like this." You wail frantically, beat yourself, tear at your skin.

"Damn it, Phyllis, cut it out! It's no big deal, just a little shit. Stop making a federal case out of it."

Finally, your energy is spent and you lie moaning. "Oh God! Oh God! I just want to die. Take me back to Magee. Take me back. I don't want anything else to happen. Please take me back."

I can't comfort you. Your shame and agony are too raw.

PHYLLIS

✳   On my night table sit the twenty-eight magnificent, one-of-every-color-I-could-imagine roses, as though every year had its own special bloom. Do they grow black roses?

In the beautiful Four Seasons Hotel room we rented to celebrate our anniversary, I shit the bed, and you, my dearest, cleaned me up lovingly and even laughingly. I cannot live with myself.

Every day I watch my roses die, one by one. Deep red roses turn blackish; pink silky ones dry up; light-peach-colored flowers dry to a yellow powder; the expensive, luscious, lavender rose fades to pale pink. Their petals all fall on my nightstand. Their death is a slow process. Not like the one instant that fatally changed our twenty-eight years of marriage.

A friend takes the petals and turns them into a sachet.

There is so little that I have to offer. As I look down at my lower body I am appalled. It is not that I covet death; I fear death. It is this helpless life that I cannot stand. I cannot move to my own desires. I sit and wait for others to come and take care of me. I feel weak and sick so much of the time. Nothing I do helps. My injured body reacts in ways I cannot understand or tolerate. Every muscle in the feeling, active part of my body hurts. I am so ugly; my stomach protrudes because I have no muscles. I hate this life, wouldn't you?

If I die, I know I will leave you lonely. That is not my intent. I love you so and I grieve at your grief. You know me well enough to know how selfish I am. This time I'm not able to beat my own image, image, image. Suicide is vanity and ego.

I cannot believe that this person in the wheelchair is me. I look down at myself and see my bottom half, legs and feet, as part of a wheelchair. I am saddened, appalled, and disgusted. I feel that I'm not real. This me that pushes around in a wheelchair is foreign. I feel ashamed and embarrassed. How will I face people I know? I dread for them to see me. I am a freak. My loss is so great. My world has been ruined. I have lost use of my legs, bladder function, body sensation, and bowel control. My life is lost. This is unreal. How can this be me? The alternative ways of managing my body are repulsive to me.

In occupational therapy the only thing I can see is the wheelchair. It looms and overshadows everything. I draw wheelchairs, the backs of people in wheelchairs, wheels instead of legs.

Through my mind's eye I watch this stranger, Phyllis. Her days at the rehab were endless and mindless. The routine was as familiar as the proverbial back of her hand: PT, OT, meals, nursing care, and learning about home care. The insanity of the whole thing drove her wild. On bad days, when that injured body acted annoyed and fatigued or in some way out of control, she could not see any humor in her plight. Her moods, feelings, and thoughts were controlled by the action of her body. When she felt ill her thoughts were low enough to make her irrationally suicidal. On the good days, when bladder, spleen, and bowel all functioned according to the new style of her body, she was a lot more rational about suicide and could even see herself adjusting to this body. There was meaning in the phrase, "not knowing your ass from your elbow," a literal meaning. The whole mind-body dichotomy took on a new dimension. After the accident her mind was not greatly affecting her body at all; her body worked on manual stimulation or by reflex. The whole thing was a pain. Learning to manage this body required all of her energy.

Learning to move without muscles below the armpits was a monumental task.

She had a big team of helpers at the rehab and sideline cheerleaders who gave great encouragement. "You've got so much guts. You are still you. You can do it if anyone can. You've got so much to give. You have so much support. You have so much going for you. You're tough." She wanted to kill them all.

Even her darling husband was sure they could have a life that was good. What was so noble in struggling to live a crippled life? She could hear it now, "Look at all she has accomplished in spite, or perhaps because, of it." Fuck that shit. Where was it written that she had to cope? On bad days she knew she didn't have to, that their wanting her to was selfish and mean. None of them cared how pained she was, how miserable her psyche felt, how trapped the wheelchair made her feel. She had something special about her. People were attracted to her and most would go an extra mile for her. She had a certain charisma. But that was no relief from pain, although it gave her pride just as her work accomplishments did. She knew that her smarts were impressive and that her ability to verbalize, clarify, and lead was far above the average person's.

In almost any group of people she had a large share of the power. She felt powerful. Her talents were many: She was artistic, able to write, able to help people. But none of that seemed to count. There was this other physically inadequate side of her; she'd always had this side. She was fat, and she felt ugly. It was those same people who told her how courageous and wonderful she could be that in another lifetime called her "fat slob" and even now thought about her being fat. And now her body was worse than ever. Living discontentedly with her body, detesting its lack of muscle, its always going to fat, was her dark side. She had felt deformed for most of her life, and now she actually was disabled, truly inadequate, and she hated herself. On the bad days, suicide, destruction of this tormenting body, loomed in every corner. She wanted to annihilate her nonfeeling lower body, to mutilate and destroy it.

It intrigued her to know that she wouldn't feel a razor or glass cutting her and that she could watch the process and not feel pain. She began to save glass bottles in her room and was thinking about getting hold of some matches.

Dr. Marx comforts me. "If you were my wife, I'd still want to be with you. I'd want your companionship."

He has sent the psychiatrist to see me, a nice man-boy whom I like. I'm a cross between Camille and Scarlett and I'm trying to seduce him even in this awful condition. Do I know why he was called in? "Yes." I'll show you how smart I am. "Dr. Marx would like to medicate me so I'm not suicidal anymore. I don't want to be medicated."

"I won't do that," he reassures me, building trust. "How do you feel?"

Smart again, showing my many facets: "I don't know if my suicidal feelings are real or playacting. But I won't do it here."

He shakes his head. All he needs is a pipe and the analysis profile would be complete.

"How can I help you? What do you think you need?"

"Nothing." I wouldn't listen to anybody. What is there to do? I stop listening. Finally, I hear him say, "In good conscience, I have to offer you a referral when you leave, okay? Bye."

My darling children say, "You have to live. You have us. We love you. We'll help you. We want the grandchildren to know you. You have so many friends and people who love you and need you."

I say, "I love you too and I am grateful for what I have, but I cannot stand the pain." I don't have the heart to tell my beloved children that I'd give them all up for that old fat body that worked.

"David, do you hate me for ruining our anniversary?"

"Dearest, stop hating yourself. You had an accident. It's not something you did. It just happened. You know I don't hate you. I love you."

"David, please climb in bed with me.

"Lying side by side is wonderful. I haven't felt this close to you for a while. I feel better now."

Sometimes during the day or night strange nurses from other floors come to my room and thank me for helping them with their families. Some come for advice about troubled kids or drunken lovers.

One has a thirteen-year-old getting ready to give birth—what's to say? Another, a runaway who seems to be in Minneapolis. I give her our office number to get help from the Toughlove group in Minneapolis. Her kid is only fifteen. Everyone has pain.

Flowers come to the nurses' station for Nurse Katy, candy the next day. Everyone is talking. "He's an older man," Nurse K. answers.

"Is he married?" suspicious me asks.

"No, I don't think so," she says mischievously wide-eyed. "Just debonair."

Nurse Laura wants to leave her husband. He doesn't talk, he's boring, she wants more, something different.

One nurse wants to be a lawyer. She's struggled to raise her kid alone, conceived when she was fifteen. She's ambitious and is applying for funds to go to school.

Marguerita and Eve both want to be models. Everyone wants something different.

Barbara's friend is a drunk and she knows he's no good. One day her eye is black. She presses charges and throws him out.

Lady Di comes in looking flushed, "Guess what?"

"I can't."

"My friend from Arizona has returned."

"Good, but be careful." I feel protective.

"Don't worry, I'm not so easy."

Dela, who is sometimes my nurse, comforts me by talking of her disability, juvenile-onset diabetes. She had to fight her nursing school to get her degree. "They had the balls to tell me after my first year," and her big blue eyes open wide, her hands on her hips, "that I might go into a diabetic coma while lifting a patient so they couldn't let me be a nurse. Can you imagine? But I fought and won. Here I am," and she twirls around, "so fight," she says. What really cheers me is when she talks of her home life.

"Now, picture this," she stops, opens her mouth and frames her face with her hands, "ready, okay, here goes . . . Christmas we gave the kids lovebirds, fine, wonderful, good birds, right?

This is February, right? So one bird drops dead on Valentine's Day and I am in my shorty nightgown, cardboard folded to scrape up the dead beast and lay it nicely in a box. Lined with a piece of velvet so my daughter shouldn't feel bad when she sees it. Then the other damn bird flies out of the cage. The kid comes in the door from outside and the bird, my luck, flies right out. "Mommy, Mommy, get it, get it,' my kids start to cry. I rush outside, it's twenty degrees and ten o'clock in the morning and I'm standing in my tiny nightgown, showing it to everyone, calling, 'Here birdie.' No answer. I figure the thing hit the cold and is dead somewhere in the snow. Well, it's gone, and yes, you guessed it, I'm locked out, freezing to death. Talk about luck.

"Bill, my husband, is upstairs, sleeping. After ten calls and throwing boulders he hears me and opens the door with, 'What the hell are you doing out there like that for?' 'I thought I'd like to flash it for the neighbors, right, what else?' I tell him. I put on my robe, ten blankets, and some tea. By now the kid notices the other bird's missing and wants to know what happened. I show her the box. The bird is in it feet-up. She closes the lid and says, 'I guess Pretty Boy went to fly to heaven to see Jasmine. Can I have a turtle, Ma?' Perfect. One day I'll tell you what happened to the dog." And in the same run-on sentence, she says, "Anyway, I'm going to leave Bill."

✳ XXIV ✳

DAVID

✳ You have asked me to bring some of your lovely clothes to the hospital. You want to see if they still fit. I have the color sense and coordination of a termite. Nevertheless I gather those clothes that match the list I have made from your descriptions. I feel as if I'm translating an article written in Latin, which I know nothing about, into English without a dictionary. I know the trying-clothes-on scene will be horrendous, but I bravely venture to Magee with your clothes.

I'm in luck. Jodi and Nitya have arrived to visit. Coward that I am, I plan my escape.

"Jodi, why don't you help Mom on with these clothes I brought. I'll take Nitya out for a walk."

"Okay, Dad," she says as I beat a hasty retreat.

PHYLLIS

✳ "**S**hut up! Stop it!" Jodi's shouting at me. I'm hysterical, tearing at my body, scratching my face. My beautiful clothes don't fit.

"I hate myself. I hate myself." I'm tearing off the clothes.

"Stop! Some things look good, Ma. All the pants fit. The pants and sweaters look good. You're just being a maniac."

"But Daddy didn't bring the matching pants to this top or the top to these pants. I can't stand it."

"So he wasn't perfect. He'll bring it next time. Candice will make you things. Dressmaker par excellence Reiko will fix your things." (I'm thinner in some places and fatter in others.)

"I look awful," narcissistic to the end. I look like a quad, classic, stereotypical, more like my fellow quads than a real person.

Tina, my nurse, sits and tells me of her desires, her bad marriage, and so on, as she watches me apply makeup: the foundation, the blush, the eye shadow, and the mascara; the lipstick I learned to use at my mother's knee. With each stroke of paint I know I will kill myself. When I'm finished, I look like a cadaver made up for her funeral. Nurses, doctors, patients, and David tell me how great I look.

"David," says Nurse Tina, "I watched Phyllis make her face come alive and heard her say all the while that she is going to kill herself. It seemed so incongruous. Which is real?"

We don't know.

Charles, the walking prisoner quad, comes into the TV lounge and sits next to me. "Charles, why don't you come to spinal cord group anymore?"

"Well, I don't have to so why bother. Anyway, I have to go to the prison ward at Jenkins Hospital with this damn halo on." He looks worried and sounds down.

"Yeah, how will you protect yourself?"

"I don't know."

"What happened to your bail, Charles?"

"It was so high the only way my mamma could raise it was to

mortgage the house and that ain't right." I think that what he really means is she won't do it.

"Okay, Charles, I'll see you in the morning."

His two police guards escort him away.

DAVID

✳ Claire from the physical therapy department and John from the occupational therapy department have come to advise me about making our house accessible.

"This hillside corner you are on is going to create difficulties," says John.

"Your driveway is steep and angular. The gravel will make any wheeling on Phyllis's part impossible," says Claire.

"You'll have to have the whole area leveled and macadamed. That cellar window will have to be covered over, the opening presents a hazard. Also the stone wall near the kitchen doors needs to be removed and the area made larger so a wheelchair can be turned in the space. You need at least a five-foot circumference," says John.

"You have to ramp the kitchen door. Remember you need one foot of ramp length for every inch you go up. Let's see," says Claire taking out a tape measure, "you've got a rise of three inches. That means you need a ramp three feet long."

On and on they go.

"Your stairway won't accommodate an electric chair glide to take Phyllis upstairs. You'll need an elevator."

"You don't have a bathroom or bedroom downstairs. You'll probably have to build one."

"The new kitchen you just put in is not usable by Phyllis. It will need to be changed."

"The slight difference in height between the living room and kitchen will either need to be ramped or one of the floors leveled."

They offer suggestions for making the house more comfortable for you but I know your aesthetic sense will be devastated. You have always been so sensitive to your surroundings. When we were first married I thought you were just a brat, but through the years I've learned it's an actual physical response you have. I know we will need a place where, at least, you are visually comfortable.

Claire and John try so hard to be helpful. Their suggestions are always tempered with, "I'd like to suggest . . ." or "I think you might find this helpful . . ."

But when I finally say, "How practical do you think it is for us to live here?" they both agree that it's not a very good location.

Tonight I tell you what Claire and John said.

"I'll put the house up for sale. Is that okay with you, Phyllis?"

"Yes. There is nothing else to do."

"I'll look around for a place to rent until we're home for a while and see what we need."

"Okay, David. You do what you think best."

"Yes, dear."

PHYLLIS

❈ Now that my halo is off I have to get ready to go home.

"You'll have to order your equipment soon."

"I don't want that equipment in my house, ugly chairs on wheels with shit buckets under them. All in vinyl, mustard-colored 1950s aqua. No taste, no class, no style. Even crips like pretty things. I can't be the only one."

"But," says Claire, "you have to be practical."

"I don't care. When we build a house I'll have a shower room right off the pool, a toilet built to be the right height and type of seat. I can picture the oriental-flowered tile room, the lovely bench I can transfer to."

"Be sure the bench is padded," warns Claire.

"But in the meantime, Phyllis, you've got to order something."

I choose the best, most modern wheelchair I can find, but I have to order an ugly potty chair from the torture chambers of the fifteenth century. I'll never forgive my PT or the medical supply houses or the manufacturers.

I can just picture a staff meeting where everyone is angry with Case #00001, C7 quad York. She is still defiant. She won't sand and stain her transfer board—the little wooden board that fits under her behind and serves as a bridge to move across from bed to wheelchair and back. "She keeps insisting that she can afford to buy a board," whines the occupational therapist. "She seems to be humiliated by this board," says the psychologist, and the physical therapist sighs, "She's so impractical." "Off with her head," yells Dr. Marx.

Today my intensive-care nurse, Kay, is here to visit from Jefferson Hospital. Jefferson is a lifetime away and I am my usual ungrateful self.

"How could you let me live? Why didn't you let me die?" jumps out of my mouth, shocking me as well as her. "I'm sorry. Forgive me, please, Kay."

"It's all right," she soothes, though her eyes reveal her pain for an instant. "It was my job to help you live and you deserve to live."

Kay was the first person to call me a "quad." I felt insulted. It was like the first time I was called a kike. But now I understand that first and foremost I'm a quad, a person in a wheelchair, disabled, crippled, handicapped, and only if they or you can keep looking or making contact might I become a real person.

Every prejudice I hold against myself I have had about the others. I will tear myself to pieces. Images haunt my psyche and talk about me, evil, crippled, disfigured people.

Richard Widmark throwing the wheelchair-bound old lady down the stairs as he laughs.

Barbara Stanwyck as the invalid in *Sorry, Wrong Number*, whining and sobbing.

The power-mad Dr. Strangelove.

The murderous, disfigured Joan Crawford in *A Woman's Face* and *Whatever Happened to Baby Jane?*

The plethora of invalided, bitter wheelchair persons demanding too much, falsifying their illness, exaggerating their helplessness, keeping others in bondage, inspiring murder or murdering.

My friend and co-worker, Teresa, whose mother was the only person to vote for Thomas E. Dewey, keeps telling me not to forget the outstanding cripples, the special ones, the athletes: so and so walking across the country on one good leg; the young man with the strong upper body wheeling himself across America for some charity.

Then there's Dr. Gillespie, wise old doc that he is, in his wheelchair rubbing his arthritic white hands.

And, last but not least, there's the late and great President of the United States, Franklin Delano Roosevelt.

"Dear Mr. President, What kept you going after the polio?"

"Those women in my life. Between my mother, Lucy, and Eleanor I got the best of care. Ho! Ho!"

"How much energy did it take for you to stand up in all those newsreels and wave to me?"

"Lots, my dear, but image is image."

Do I have to commit murder, be murdered, become infamous or heroic, an old lady wheeling her way across America to show that the lame care about the poor?

My social worker, like others around me who try to fulfill my needs and desires, to help make me happier, healthier, more "able" as they say, brings me information about stylish clothes for the handicapped. I cannot bear it! I want Candice's elegant clothes designs.

And like magic, after David leaves, Candice appears. I hear the high-heeled boots click to a stop outside my door. She brings the cold snowy night and the excitement of New York's garment center right into my room in her portfolio.

She has the nerve to wear her new sable coat down here.

"How do you like it? It's not quite finished, but I wanted to show it to you. Do you like it, do you?"

How could I not? Her blunt-cut long black hair is moving from side to side as she turns round and round.

We try on some clothes. "What's happened to you? Where are the titties?" They've fallen. Little apples they never were, but now they are spread out like a desert Arab's goat's or cowhide water pouches that are half empty.

Candice makes me cry.

"Don't cry, darling, don't cry," she soothes. "We'll fix it, darling."

On with soft and hard jackets, silk blouses, jersey ones, cotton, all of the clothes she has schlepped here.

"Your shoulders are smaller. You don't need man-tailored clothes. Don't worry, we'll fix everything. I'll tell Reiko. Look, darling, I've started something for you. See this jacket, wonderful white canvas full at the bottom. You'll look marvelous. You'll be like a queen; everyone will wait on you. It's not so bad to be a queen."

"But I can't walk," I'm crying.

"Shush, darling, they'll carry you. You'll have to work out. Look at my arm." And she made a muscle. She works out three times a week at a weight-lifter's gym.

"My asthma is almost gone since I've been working out," she tells me.

"Do you think my quadraplegia will leave if I work out?"

"Working out is good, but not that good," she laughs. "I have to go, darling, Purvis is meeting me for dinner so I can drop the Jag off at the garage."

The last thing I see is the full sable flashing out the door.

I'm tired, but happier. "Good night, dear. I'm glad Ilene's coming this weekend, she'll bring me clothes that match."

I awake in the middle of the night thinking about how shallow I am. All this business with clothes. I can never leave my self alone.

"Mary, how come I'm so shallow? All I care about is how I look, how fat I am."

Mary's view of my behavior is always different from mine. She will not beat me up.

"Being fat is an old normal concern, something you are used to, something easier to deal with than what has happened. Yet it shows concern with your body. You are also a very visual person. You paint and draw. What you see is important to you; you are aesthetic."

"Thanks, Mary I'm no longer shallow, I'm aesthetic."

"Death can be a reasonable alternative to some existences," I intellectualize to my doctor.

Dr. Marx tells me, "You want to kill yourself because you are depressed."

"I can kill myself without being depressed."

"You will function like a para, not a quad. You will not be disabled. You have good function. You will have a good life."

What does he know? He's used to crips.

"Look, you stick to medicine, I'll take care of my psyche. Get out."

"You're no different than you were before the accident. You're the same person you always were."

"How can you say that? I've lost my body, my ability to walk, to feel."

"Yeah, but you are the same person—the same inside."

"I'm different. Others will see me differently. My body is me and I am different—someone I don't know, a thing."

Later in group thereapy, I bring it up. The group reproaches like a Greek chorus, "That's not all of you."

"Phyllis is right. Sure, our bodies make us changed. But I can see Sam's point too. Inside we're the same."

Hooray, it's Valiant, disguised as Carl Rogers, the master of diplomacy, peacemaker, counselor.

"People will treat you differently."

"Yeah, they'll grab your chair and think they're helping when they push you in the wrong direction," says a patient who has been injured for several years.

"They avoid your eyes," says another.

I'm thinking, who cares about what others think, if I don't think it too?

Later Anne, the psychologist, comes to my room and assures me that I'm not the only one who feels the way I do. "It's that you're more verbal."

"I've noticed."

Sometimes I think, "Was I ever anyone else? I have always been this person that is now in a wheelchair and I resent accepting this."

Sometimes I see myself taking for granted my having to weight-shift, and I resent the acceptance.

After our day's work in physical therapy and occupational therapy, a few of us meet in the hall near the nurses' station and talk. Some of us wheel our wheelchairs with our hands since we are unable to use our legs; others move their chairs with their feet since they are unable to use their arms.

A nurse places a letter in Lloyd's forever closed fingers which soon manages to fall to the floor. Valiant pushes the letter with his feet over to a para who picks it up and passes the letter to me. I pass the letter to Ike who places it in Lloyd's wheelchair. It seems the five of us make one useful body. Next time we'll ask a nurse to pick up the letter.

DAVID

✳   "Phyllis, I will be away in Baltimore for a Toughlove weekend workshop. I've asked people to visit while I'm gone. Jodi and Nitya will be here on Saturday as usual. Heidi, Christopher, and Ian will be here on Sunday. Also, Alan said he will take you out to dinner since Gwen will be in Baltimore at the workshop."

"I'll be okay, David. You don't need to make plans for me, but thanks anyway."

Again, I'm reminded how much of Phyllis's life belongs to Magee. I'm not sure I like trading in guilt for jealousy.

XXV

PHYLLIS

❋ Alan and his daughter Stacy take me on an outing while you're away in Baltimore. Stacy is almost thirteen and can be embarrassed at the drop of a hat. Alan laughs and Stacy says, "Shh." Alan eats a lot and Stacy says, "Oh, Daddy."

I have found out something wonderful, dear. I have regained my ability to eat chocolate!

After Alan had driven up on the sidewalk to let me out of the car because there was no curb cut for the wheelchair, we stopped at a candy store next to the restaurant where we were having dinner. He bought me one chocolate truffle to try. I bit off a small piece and sucked it slowly into my mouth. No choking, sputtering, no shortness of breath. I ate a larger piece, waited, and finished off the truffle. No pain, just pure ecstasy.

Alan bought me truffles of every kind, champagne, orange, vanilla, caramel, raspberry, chocolate, chocolate rum. I ate at least two of each variety. Maybe life will be worth living.

Lifting me out of the car after our outing, Alan steps on my pee bag and fills his shoe with urine. Life is complete.

DAVID

❈ At the weekend workshop in Baltimore I've asked Jimmy, a young man who came to our very first weekend workshop in 1981, to fill in. Jimmy is a lay minister who has started parent Toughlove groups in Holmesburg, Pennsylvania. He went to divinity school, decided not to be ordained, and returned to his hometown of Holmesburg to work with kids. Like most of us who start with kids, Jimmy believed that being a helping friend who earned a kid's trust was the answer. When this ploy didn't work, Jimmy started working with parents just at the time our first Toughlove weekend workshop was given. He has been a believer and hard worker for us ever since. With all of this, Jimmy is still an unknown quantity as far as helping with our current workshop.

Jimmy, Gwen, Teresa, and I have gone over the various tasks each of us will do and worked out our role plays. Teresa and I will do the "window story." I'll be the sixteen-year-old who screams obscenities at his elderly mother who rushes around closing windows so the neighbors won't hear. Teresa will be the mother who gives into this tyrannical behavior out of helplessness. I'm not sure Teresa can pull off the punch line of finally opening the windows and telling all her neighbors to listen to her foul-mouthed child calling her an old fucking scumbag. The role play is such a good one that I hope we can make it work.

Sunday evening, after the workshop, I call you. "Hi, Phyllis, how are you, my dear?"

"Hello, David, I'm fine. I had a good time going out with Alan and Stacy. Best of all, my body has reconciled its digestive difficulties with chocolate and I pigged out. But how was the workshop?"

"The workshop went well. As I expected but hoped wouldn't

happen, it was more mechanical than if you had been there. Luckily the format we've developed over the years is super. The audience loved it. They were all enthusiastic and ready to go back home and go to work."

"How did Jimmy, Gwen, and Teresa work out?"

"Jimmy was super. His ministerial style goes over great. He prances back and forth on the stage preaching the gospel according to Toughlove. He sells more of our books than we do.

"The window story turned out to be hilarious, not by design, but by default. Teresa and I did our act all the way to the end. I kept saying to her, like the sixteen-year-old we based the skit on, 'Give me the car keys, you old fuck! You'd better give them to me, you old scumbag,' but Teresa just stood there. Finally I asked her what she was waiting for and she told me, 'To call me an old *fucking* scumbag.' I was flabbergasted and then realized she needed that exact sequence of words. I got the magic words out while choking with laughter. Teresa was galvanized into action and pretended to open windows while shouting, 'Listen, neighbors, listen to what my son is calling me. He is calling me an old,' and she hesitated, 'scumbag.' The 'F' word stuck in her throat. It was great fun. Grandparents in the audience shared their own pain and helplessness. One couple, in particular, were heartrending when they discussed their fifteen-year-old daughter and their grandson. The daughter acts as if the kid belongs to them while she continues to run the streets. The group rallied around them and they made some plans to begin confronting their daughter.

"Gwen did a good job on the blame game. She shared the story of how her family plays Sherlock Holmes in trying to find out who did it. No one in the family will take on the role of Dr. Watson to keep things straight so everyone ends up accusing everyone else. Eventually the problem gets lost and everyone feels vindicated, blamed, and angry all at the same time."

"I'm glad it went well, David. I miss you. Hurry home."

"I miss you too, my dear. I'll be in to see you tomorrow."

PHYLLIS

✳   I'm trying and trying to do intermittent catheterization again—I tap in the bladder area and get sores from tapping—every four hours. I'm sick. My pressure goes up and they have to catheterize me, more and more. My pressure is killing me: stroke high, 150/100 to 250/180 and so on. I even wake up with it high. I can't function. I don't want to give in to a permanent catheter.

Sometimes my blood pressure drops to 60/40 and I'm so tired I cannot function. I couldn't get out of my room today. Dr. Marx says, "Wear a binder around your stomach. Wear Teds [elastic stockings]. They will stop your blood from pooling."

The binder makes sores and marks on me. The Teds make me feel like an old lady. Sometimes they help, but not always.

DAVID

❊ Returning from Baltimore, I find you in your room letting the water in the sink run over your hands. You look so pale and exhausted. You smile and whisper, "I've missed being able to wash my hands or even feel the water flowing over them." I, who like to wash the dishes because of the pleasure I feel in immersing my hands in hot, soapy water, feel a pang of pain. You tell me, "I'm trying intermittent catheterization again. I can't stand not even being able to control my bladder."

"I understand, my dear, but it's not worth dying for."

"This injury hasn't left me much to live for."

"Stop it, Phyllis. You know you have a lot to live for."

"Yeah, yeah. Just leave me alone, David."

"No, I won't."

"I'm too tired to fight."

"Me too."

The rest of the visit passes in silence. I wish I were back in Baltimore.

PHYLLIS

❊ Katy has just cathed me and my blood pressure has dropped and I'm not me. I'm one of those detectives in an old private-eye movie, the ones where the dick gets hit on the head by a mysterious hand that just rifled his office, or gets slipped a Mickey Finn by a not-so-friendly bartender.

I'm like Sam Spade starting to come to. The whole silver screen is wavy. I'm saying something like, "Everything is moving around." I'm locked in a car that just fell over a bridge. I'm watching myself float around underwater with the rest of the fish. But I'm not underwater. I'm just back in my own bed trying to figure out what day it is.

As she dresses me, Katy says, "It's just your blood pressure. Your body hasn't learned to work out the new logistics yet."

I head downstairs to physical therapy but by the time I get there I'm feeling awful, out of it. My pressure is up; I see spots and stars. Katy comes and gets me and we rework the script of *Gone With the Wind* while she catheterizes me.

"I never birthed no babies, Miz Scarlett," she intones as she prepares the catheter.

"You better birth this one," I hiss in a whispering Scarlett voice. But quickly I transform into the wonderful, forgiving, loving Melanie. "It's okay, darlin' Scarlett, I'll be just fine. But if I should die from lack of pissing, I leave wonderful David York in your care. I trust you, even if you put the make on him every time I am indisposed." Nurse doing Scarlett says, "Hush up, now Melanie. You ain't gonna die," as urine runs out of the catheter. My blood pressure plummets and I become the dying Camille giving a farewell speech.

Dr. Marx knocks at the door and walks onto our stage. Nurse Scarlett hastily covers my private parts with a sheet to protect me from this man who has stared at the bedsore on my behind for the last ten weeks.

"You're very depressed today?"

"No, just unhappy."

(I think this must be the twice-a-week team meeting time with reports from PT, OT, Psych, and Nursing.)

"Your pressure will give you a stroke. You'll get used to a leg bag. You cannot do this, you're making yourself sick. No more intermittent catheterization, okay?"

And just because he says "Okay?" I say, "No, I'll wait till morning."

"I'm not giving another penny to ERA. All you women like is power," and he leaves.

I am starting the BAG—a forever plastic tube and urine bag down my leg. I smell of rubber tubing and plastic, and alcohol swabs are my perfume. I want to die.

DAVID

❋ My visits to the hospital are dreadful. You are in a constant funk. Your blood pressure is running all over the place and your urine isn't running at all. At least it isn't running where and when and how it should. Lying on your stomach, the pressure on the bladder forces the urine out. This means a trip upstairs to wash, change, and catheterize to make sure all the urine is voided. Meanwhile, your blood pressure bottoms out to 60/40, hardly enough to stay alive. You're so out of it that you're hallucinating. We both keep hoping your bladder will respond.

This can't keep up. You, my poor, dear Phyllis, must accept another permanent indignity. I tell you we can try later when you get stronger. I'm so relieved and guilty for being relieved when I see the permanent urine bag attached. Now, at least, my nightly laundry runs can diminish to normal.

PHYLLIS

❋ Ike is walking in braces holding onto parallel bars. He's strong—he can even transfer in and out of a car. I see his equipment has come in—a potty chair and shower chair in one; he's ordered his wheelchair. He plans to go back to live on campus. He's much braver than I am. He and his parents come over to say good-bye. He gives me his phone number.

Now it's my turn to get ready to go home. Like Jennifer said and Ike denies and Aleta cries, I am scared. I don't want this life.

Valiant is staying a while longer, his hands are stronger and he can propel his chair with one leg. Walking may be an option . . .

I am jealous of dear Valiant.

Help, help! My goddamn behind is taped to the railings of my bed in an effort to get me off my bedsore so it can heal.

Every time I'm turned in bed I'm taped and retaped. The tape hangs off the railings of my bed like funeral crepe that decorates the parish church at the death of the priest. Still my sore does not heal.

"You need to be off the sore. We'll try to prone-cart," says Dr. Marx.

"Oh, no!"

"Yes! Yes! Five to ten days on a cart and you'll stay on for six hours a day. Okay?"

I say, "No, no," but I'll do it.

This is the final insult, you goddamned body. Do I have to experience everything?"

"I hate it, David."

"I know you do, but the sore has to heal."

Being on the gurney, flat on my belly, is a killer. My neck hurts from trying to look up; my arms are killing me from wheeling and weight-shifting in this position, but my butt is improving. Now I understand why all those young men lying around on carts are high all the time. There is only one way to tolerate this position in life and that's stoned out of my gourd on pot. On the veranda, day in and day out, good friends help me stay high, until my behind is almost healed.

I am sick and tired of practicing for my life as a quad. I cannot stand one more discussion of, "What will it be like out there?" or "Is there anything orgasmic after spinal cord injury?"

"Dr. Marx, I'm going home on Wednesday."

"It's too soon, you have to wait a week for your equipment, beds, and other stuff."

"Okay."

"Are you sure you don't want to stay one month more and learn more, get stronger?"

"I'll learn at home. I'm not going to physical therapy or occupational therapy much any more. I have my exercise routine now. I can roll over and sit up. I need to practice transferring but I can do all these things at home. I have to wear a leg bag, so . . ."

"Okay, we'll get you ready."

None of my equipment is here because I've taken so long to accept the fact that I need it. I'll go home with rented monstrosities. David, Gwen, and Teresa all hear about my leaving. Together they're excited—they're worried I won't like the house we rented.

David, I can't sleep anymore. Every time the night nurses come in I'm sitting up in the middle of the bed. Some interesting talk shows are on at four to five in the morning. It's time for me to come home. I'm through sleeping here.

I watch the long-injured or born-hurt. Their life and attention is focused on their helplessness, on doctors, nurses, OTs, and PTs. No time for the ordinary neighbor except to talk about themselves and their body needs.

Anne, dear psychologist, "Will I become like them?"

And from her own polio life Anne tells me, "No, that style of crippled being belongs only to the early institutionalized. First, I was a crippled person, then just very special, always watching where my bread was buttered. Later, I had to learn to be just a person," she explains.

✻ XXVI ✻

PHYLLIS

✻ We're in Bloomingdale's and God, dearest, how I love you to push my wheelchair fast! It's fun. The lovely things, the colors are a treat for my eyes; the textures of the clothes please me, and best of all are the smells of the cosmetics and perfume counters. I hate being smaller than everyone and not seeing or reaching the tops of counters or racks, but the pure sensuousness of the experience makes up for the losses. "Isn't Bloomie's wonderful."

"Yes, but seeing you so happy is even better."

"David, stop here at the hats. I want to buy one for Stacy's confirmation." I try on at least five. I like a straw hat with a bow and veil that comes over my eyes a little.

David tells me, "You look supersexy and beautiful." So we buy it.

We also buy presents for Lady Di and Barbara.

You are so giving. You enjoyed my buying the straw hat with the bow and veil for Stacy's Bat Mitzvah. You encourage me to be decadent.

Lady Di squeals, "Oh, look what I got!" as she shows everyone the beach bag we got her for her trip. Lady Di is going to California after I leave.

This morning I gave Barbara, who has become very dear to me, her blouse. She liked it.

It's hard parting even though I want to leave.

I'm going home, going home, going home, going home. I'm going home, going home, on this warm day April 4, 1984.

I'm going home just like this!

I'm scared.

"Phyllis, have you got everything?" asks the head nurse as she runs down the hated list:

the leg bags—for daytime peeing

Chux—to cover the bed against bowel and bladder mishaps

wheelchair—for mobility

night bags—large, for nighttime peeing

Foley kits by the case—the permanent catheters to change every few weeks

shower chair—to sit on in the shower

leg bands—to hold catheter tubes in place

three different medications to produce bowel movements

plastic gloves—to cover my finger when I stimulate my anal sphincter to trigger bowel movements.

"I've ordered your bed with rails. The Upjohn nurse will come to the house. You're lucky you could rent a house."

Here's David. "You ready, dearest? I'll load the car!" We exchange kisses and hugs.

"Good-bye," I say to all. "Don't cry," warn the nurses and aides as they wipe their eyes. No one's address do I take, as I promise to keep in touch and we're in the car.

"Phyllis, I hope you like the house."

"I will, don't worry. What color are the rugs?"

You don't remember. I don't really care. I'm scared and you're scared but happy to have me home. We're quiet for a while and then I ask, "How do I live like this? I can't do it. I don't know how. I don't want to do it."

"Phyllis, you haven't even tried yet. You don't know what it's like. You'll do it by living it. Give us time. At least we'll have each other, a house and . . ."

"Oh, shut up."

"You too."

DAVID

✳ Phyllis is coming home, coming home. She is coming home, coming home on a warm April 4, 1984, day.

She is coming home just the way she is.

I'm scared.

Phyllis's sensitivity to her surroundings worries me. Will she like the colors on walls, floors, ceilings, or will it drive her crazy? Long ago I gave up buying gifts for Phyllis, they were never right. We ended up shopping together. It worked out better for both of us.

Now, Phyllis is coming home to a house I rented on my own. I've done the practical, brought a wheelchair to the house and made sure we can get into the front door, bedroom, bathroom, and kitchen. There are some tight squeezes but it can be done. A wonderful friend of ours, Paul Hogan, who goes all around the world helping kids build playgrounds, has built a long ramp so we can navigate the two steps into the house. He also built a ramp so Phyllis can use the backyard. Our landlord is so nice I can't believe it. I needed to remove a bathroom door and take off some of the wood trim and they insisted I go ahead and do what I had to. I feel really pleased with all the arrangements I've made. I hope she'll like it. We don't have any other options.

PHYLLIS

✳ The house in the suburbs is more attractive than I expected, a lovely secluded backyard, old heavy trees, and a swimming pool. The house, a sixties rancher, is fine for now. Enough room for me and my equipment and the Toughlove business too. Teresa and Gwen will work in the full basement. There's enough space there for each to have an office for herself, storage room for our books, and tables for preparing the packages of materials we sell to support ourselves and our Toughlove group.

Flowers from a friend greet me at the door. The place is bare, only our two twin hospital-style Craftmatic rail-on-my-side beds have arrived. There will be a crack between the two beds, separating us.

David brings in the supples to aid our new life.

"Come on, we'll have dinner in town," he suggests. I'm tired but I say okay.

DAVID

✳ We need more medical supplies. Magee supplied us with a little bit of everything.

I find the medical supply store tremendously depressing. Wheelchairs, toilet chairs, walkers, special beds, electric carts, and myriad prosthetic paraphernalia fill the store and remind me of our new life. I am embarrassed to be here. It is my public declaration that I have one of "these people." I don't want to be in a place like this. I don't want to need these supplies. I want life to return to normal. Phyllis and I are going to live the same life we had before this accident.

We have Stacy's Bat Mitzvah to attend and many dinner dates with friends who have been waiting to see us. The wheelchair is just an inconvenience. I'll manage.

You like the house. Hooray. I feel everything is coming together. We can manage. Nurses will be coming to get you up, put you to bed, and help in the afternoon. We've got the toilet chair, shower chair, and wheelchair. We have a small room loaded with all kinds of extra equipment and the necessary supplies. Barring World War III, we are ready for anything.

PHYLLIS

Home on Thursday and to Stacy's Bat Mitzvah on Saturday. I'm happy to be there and see this lovely child come of age and recognize the goodness of her parents. It's the first time I've ever seen Alan—the dentist, the husband, the father, the friend, the pilot, the hunter who loves stuffed trophies, big ugly belt buckles, and lots of great food—dressed in a suit. He looks like a Bar Mitzvah boy himself. He makes me smile. Gwen is gorgeous in mauve and pink. Stacy's performance is flawless.

The reception is like Gwen and Alan—generous, sumptuous, well-ordered, and a little outrageous.

DAVID

The Bat Mitzvah is lovely. Phyllis looks great. She is wearing an off-white silk suit with lace at the throat, topped off by the terrific-looking hat we bought at Bloomingdale's. She is treated like royalty on a movable throne. But it's downhill from here on. Her catheter comes out and I haven't thought to bring an extra from the roomful of supplies we have at home. Local drugstores don't carry such exotic stuff so our daughter Ilene goes on a catheter hunt. Phyllis needs a secluded place to lie down, so three of us haul her up ten stairs to a bedroom. Meanwhile, panicsville; I have visions of dysreflexia marching inexorably on. Phyllis gets through to me, "Look, David, relax, I'm not in any trouble. We can use the old catheter until Ilene returns. I'll just have to stay here and not move." Whew! saved. I feel relief as the yellow flows again.

Ilene returns, the catheter is in, and back down the ten steps we go. The celebration is going wonderfully. Our crisis dampened no one's spirits. When it's time to go home I have three small steps to navigate. Usually I get three people to help but everyone is into the party so I figure I can do it with the help of one person. On the third step I slip and Phyllis hits the floor with the back of her head. What have I done? How could I let this happen? I know that if I've caused any further injury Phyllis will kill herself for sure. If that happens I won't be able to live with myself. The party stops as people crowd around. I'm devastated. Alan picks Phyllis up and checks her out. Thank God, she's okay. A little tingling in her fingers but everything is still moving. Alan puts his arm around me and sternly tells me to let him help next time.

Appropriately chastised and feeling terrible, I head home from our first outing.

I can't do it!
I can't do it!
I'm making our life miserable by trying to make it better. I'm pushing Phyllis to go and do everything.
I didn't do it.
But I'll make it better next time.
I'll work harder. I'll be more responsible. I won't make a mistake.
I can do it!
We've been invited out to dinner every night for the past week. Phyllis is tired but I'm sure she'll get over it. We have so many people who want to welcome us home. Finally one night, when we're ready to go out, Phyllis says, "I can't do it, David, I'm just too tired."

"How can you say this now? We've got people waiting for us. Come on, we won't stay long."

"David, I can't. I'm just too tired. I need to go to bed."

"What! It's only seven o'clock. You can't go to bed now."

"I won't go. If you want to go by yourself go ahead. I'll have the nurse come early. Go! Get out!"

I'm furious. "I won't stand up our friends just because you're a wimp. I'm leaving."

I storm out to a dinner that tastes like straw and company fit for a funeral.

When I come home you are sitting where I left you. Your face is streaked with tears and you're just slumped over. I hold you in my arms crying, "I'm sorry, I'm sorry. What have I been doing to you? I'm so thoughtless. Please forgive me. I keep acting like you're not injured. I know you can't do it."

We can't do it.
We can't do it.
I've got to remember these lessons:

❋

We can't keep living our life like we used to.

I can't keep denying that our life will never be the same again.

PHYLLIS

❋ I've been home a week. David is out at a restaurant and I am sitting looking at my dressing table, wanting to kill myself. I cannot live the old life he wants and he hates me. I hate him.

I've been to twelve restaurants, cried with everyone I've met, sold our old house, picked out furniture, gone to PT at the local hospital, gotten dropped three times not including down the steps by David. I'm wild with my own incompetence, inadequacy, and dependence. Up to now I've met a secret goal that has kept suicide at bay. During the night I can turn myself over without waking David. I could not bear to impose myself on him at night.

I'm sitting and crying, angrily looking for a way out, and David comes home. "I'm sorry I've been pushing you. I've been frantic to make our life just what it was. I know you can't do it," he tells me. "Okay," I say. But inside me I am planning my death.

"I'm so glad you're here with me." David holds me in his arms in the best way we can manage.

"Are you sure you want me?" I feel so unlovable, so damaged, so internally obsessed, so isolated, so pained. I relish the reassurance.

"I have you here and that's what counts," he says, but as the days go on, I see I am a task and a burden. The doctor says that David has high blood pressure. It's my fault. He gets me up, he helps dress me, cleans my pee bag, feeds me, lifts me, gets me ready for bed. How can I ask for the extra drink of water, the extra turn? When I do it's never the right time. "For Christ's sake, do you have to wait till I'm just about sitting down?" So I wait next time till he gets up to do something else or it's in the middle of something and as nonabrasively as I can I say, "When you're finished, would you please get me my glasses?"

"Please, Phyllis, stop asking for something else when I'm in the middle of taking care of a chore," he gripes at me.

"When is the right time? You're either doing something or

---

you're about to sit, or you've just sat. Well, there is no good time. I'll need something always. I'm never going to be finished and if you don't relax and stop, we can forget it!" I'm crying and screaming. David is quiet.

Later in bed, he turns to me, holds my hand, and says, "Phyllis, there's just so much to do."

"I know. I'm sorry." I think I am going to spend the rest of my life apologizing and crying.

At the crack of dawn, David says, "Yes, I need to relax and I'll try to be less demanding."

"David, will you make love to me?"

"Yes, my darling."

"I want you to." We are klutzes—but we manage, with me on my stomach. It was always my favorite position anyway.

"David, it feels pretty good, I am pleased. Really, I have good feelings at the edge of my stomach. How was it for you?"

"A pleasure," you say and smile.

My catheter fell out, but I didn't pee or shit. I wonder what he doesn't say aloud.

Sex without orgasm—the perfect metaphor. I am diminished. Life is less pleasurable, more trouble.

DAVID

✳   Sex is a perfect symbol for our new life.

I find it hard to switch from caretaker to lover. I struggle with feelings that getting laid is like helping you get dressed, getting you comfortable in bed, getting you into your wheelchair, assisting with your bowel program, your catheter, washing you. We cuddle, but for you to touch my penis, I need to do some contortions. Your normal feeling is above your armpits although you get pleasurable sensations in your vagina and, oddly enough, in your lower stomach. When we both feel ready, I need to move you on your stomach, stretch your lower leg out straight and fold your upper leg toward your chest. I check out your catheter to make sure it is not pulled taut or in the way. Now we are set. With a little luck the physical exertion hasn't made me lose my erection. If so, we start again. Intercourse involves some twists and turns. You try hard to be a physical participant and I try hard to help you enjoy our sex. My orgasm is reminiscent of our early sex life. I come and feel satisfied while you are left unfulfilled. Now I switch from lover to caretaker again and help you wash. Yes, sex is a metaphor for our life. No longer can we enjoy spontaneity. We are learning to enjoy what we have.

"How was it, David? Did you enjoy yourself?"

"Yeah, it was good. How was it for you?"

"It was okay. I get good feelings. I especially like feeling your penis swelling before you come. Do you feel any movement from me?"

"Yeah, a little. Most of it is in your shoulders though."

Tearfully you say, "I wish I could have orgasms. I miss the release."

"I wish you could too, my dear."

I feel inadequate and unfulfilled.

✳ XXVII ✳

DAVID

✳   We have too many nurses working for us. They're helpful but they interfere with the flow of our life. No matter how we schedule them, Phyllis needs something when no nurse is available. We decide to manage with only one nurse helping Phyllis shower and do her bowel program at night. On weekends I'll do it all. The luxury of being on our own schedule for at least two days is worth it. It means I'll have to do more, but what the hell, I can do it. But Phyllis knows better. "David, we cannot manage without someone to take care of the house and me. Be realistic, dear. The weekends will be enough for us to do alone. I don't want you to do everything. It will make me feel more like a burden."

"You're right, Phyllis. We'll put an ad in the paper and see if we can hire someone."

On Friday Jodi and Nitya come to visit and help out. When I tell Jodi of our plan she perks up and says, "How about hiring me? I'm sick of working at the health food store."

"Can you do the job with Nitya around?" asks Phyllis.

"Well if you don't mind her around."

Phyllis and I both agree that we'd like Nitya around. "But, we do have to work and you'll have to keep Nitya out of our way."

"I'm sure I can do it. I have Nitya at the health food store and it's no problem there."

"Jodi, are you sure you won't mind emptying my leg bag or putting me on the toilet?"

"I've done all these things already, Ma. Don't forget I even learned to cath you in the hospital."

PHYLLIS

✳   Jodi has come to be my attendant and to manage the household chores. She helps me wash and dress, and she cleans my bedsore with peroxide. She shops, cleans, and prepares David's favorite foods. She is capable and trustworthy. The problem is we are still mother and daughter and there are those days when it shows.

"You could ask me nice," she says.

"I'm grouchy. It's nothing personal against you," I say.

"You don't have to be nasty."

"Leave me alone."

Nitya watches us wide-eyed. Nitya is so pleasurable and so demanding.

Occasionally, Nitya becomes my rival. I need to get in bed, she needs to be put to sleep. I need my leg bag emptied, she needs to be diapered. I need to get into my wheelchair, she needs to eat. She refuses to come to me and says loud and clear, "No, Grandma."

Most of the time Nitya and I are buddies. I play dollies, put together puzzles, or read to her. We have a special game we play when I'm in bed. We are bunny rabbits having a tea party. When David and I are writing on the dining room table she sits and scribbles on note pads. She warms my heart and forces me to want to live.

DAVID

✳ Phyllis's energy level is zilch. Getting out of bed and eating breakfast tires her. We write at our kitchen table; we're putting together a self-help manual for people who care about a cocaine user. After an hour her neck and shoulders are so painful she can't work anymore. By three in the afternoon Phyllis is so tired she needs to get in bed. Her lack of stamina and energy forces tears of frustration from her eyes.

PHYLLIS

✳ When David's away I feel that I am dead. No matter how hard Jodi tries to comfort me, I am numb with fear. "It's wrong to kill yourself," she says from her religious heart. "You scare me," she says from her child self. "You need to visualize your self healing," she counsels from her adult self and offers visualizations for me to try. With her talented hands she massages my hurting neck, shoulders, arms, and hands. I love her and I want her to shut up.

Everyone comes to keep me company, Heidi, Ilene, the little kids. Friends sleep over to relieve Jodi. People call. I feel that I'm in a fog. I spill my hurt and pain to my nurse, who comforts me. She says this is the hardest time; hang in. "The first two years after a trauma like yours are the most difficult."

I am like the blooming dogwood tree outside my door that is slowly strangling, invaded by the weed vine that chokes it.

My suicide plan is simple. I will take all of the pills that are in the house, the Valium for muscle relaxation, the Benadryl for middle-ear nonsense, the booze for parties. I've checked out my ability to reach everything. The booze is on the first shelf in the kitchen bottom cabinet and easy to get. The pills are in my bathroom medicine closet high up on the top shelf, but with my handy-dandy reacher, the kind old-fashioned grocers used for getting the canned fruit, canned vegetables, or cereal boxes from their top shelves, it's easy.

Whenever David is away he calls me every night, "Hello, my darling, how are you?" Tears stream down my face and I manage a quiet, "Okay, how's the workshop?" "Good, good," you say and tell me some details. I'm just interested in keeping you on the line so your voice can protect me.

"Sleep cradled in my love," we say. "Come home, David," I plead. "Soon, dearest, and again sleep cradled in my love."

I remember working with a client named Madelaine who was recovering from alcoholism. One evening she came to me and said that in the quiet of the night when fear enveloped her and her urge to drink became unbearable she thought of me and held on to my image. As she spoke she picked up a small rock painted with a butterfly design from my desk and asked if she could keep it as a symbol of me. I hoped I would not fail her. One year later Madelaine returned my rock.

I want to keep David in my pocket now.

Hal came by the house the other day to let me know that Brucker, the biofeedback man in Florida, would see me. We talked of suicide. He said he spoke with one of the gurus of family therapy about me who said that I had the right to try to kill myself and others had the right to stop me.

"Mazel tov," I say, "we're at a standstill."

In my mind I am instantly transported to the office of Dr. Carl Rogers, the father of modern American psychotherapy.

"Dr. Rogers, I want to kill myself."

Pregnant pause.

The good doctor shakes his head slightly, almost imperceptibly looks at me, leans forward at about a forty-five-degree angle, and says, "You want to kill yourself?"

"Yes," I answer, and he leans back and says, "How do you feel about that?" and I answer, "Just terrific, Doc, how the hell do you think I feel?"

And he in his perceptual wisdom says, "You sound really angry." I turn and wheel out.

DAVID

✻ Traveling to do Toughlove without Phyllis leaves me ambivalent.

I look forward to getting away by myself.
There is only me to get on a plane.
There is only me to dress, wash, care for.
There is only me to get to bed.
I get up on my time schedule.
I eat on my schedule.
I take care of my needs while I work.
I don't worry about stairs, seats, access, rooms, toilets.
But I'm lonely.
I miss the company.
I miss the energy.
I miss the insight, laughter, love, and sharing.
I look forward to coming home.

Toughlove is starting to move. Our new address is becoming the norm. Our manuals and Bantam paperbacks all have the mailing change.

"Phyllis, I'm nervous about the Indianapolis workshop. My laid-back style really needs your energy and personal touch. Besides, there is no way to replace your insight and intuitive leaps. I miss our bantering and playing off each other in front of the audience. I'll miss you."

You start to cry, "David, I already miss you and I'm scared to be without you. Don't go."

"I know you agonize over my leaving, my darling, but you'll be all right. Jodi and Nitya are staying for the weekend and Ilene may come from Washington."

After you have picked out and color-coordinated my clothes, I pack and get ready to leave, and you go through your litany.

"Be careful. Don't let anything happen to you. Call me as soon as you get there. Don't be nervous, you'll do a great job. Be careful."

This is our forty-eighth Toughlove weekend workshop. I have done the last four by myself and the original design we developed continues to work well. I'm always concerned that I will get jaded and lose my spontaneity. But each group that attends the workshop brings its own problems and personalities which makes the experience totally different. Indianapolis is no exception.

Nevertheless we all miss you terribly. We resolve to get you going with us as soon as possible. We won't allow you to wimp out on us (I hope).

—— ✳ XXVIII ✳ ——

PHYLLIS

✳ A workshop is scheduled for July and as the time nears, Teresa keeps repeating, "Phyllis, that policeman who keeps saying 'How's my little gal?' "—she means the one who was at the Indiana workshop—"he wants you to come to Tulsa. He insists he'll get a van for you. They've already made sure the hotel is accessible." She pauses—she's really pushing.

Gwen picks up the slack, "It's still a long way off; you might want to try it, you don't have to go, but if you want to, I'll come, to help, we'll hire a nurse."

They're squeezing me. I am surrounded by these loyal manipulators who feel it's their duty to get me up and going.

"I am not going." But the bug's in my ear.

"I'm afraid." I don't say it, but "Maybe it's better than staying home without David and everyone" is floating around in my head. I wonder what they'll do next.

My nurse Ellen is already dear to me because she is kind, competent, and shares the world of her family with me. I feel I know her children. I admire the attention she gives to the world of her children. Her relationship with her husband seems as close as David's and mine. She is a first-class mother; she wishes her little one had another teacher but helps him to cope with the one he has. "It won't hurt you," she says, "to write your name in the right-hand corner."

She's teaching her daughter to drive and is firm about the need for her to practice so she can develop good driving judgment. She is a thoughtful person.

I share myself with her, especially the daily agonies. She does not embarrass me. So when I am tired, I let her wash me. When my hands don't work, it's okay for her to help change my tampon.

She encourages me to go to Tulsa.

Sitting at the table in the dining room, I try to work and people meet with me about business. The phone rings and it is the other David, the cop from Tulsa. He wants to know, "Is his little gal coming to Tulsa?" Teresa tells him I'm right in the room. He insists on talking to me. "Well, you're comin' down here. We're waitin' for ya. I've got it all set."

"I'll come, but you'll be sorry."

"No, I won't," and he lets out a western "Ya-hoo!" Teresa and Gwen are smiles from ear to ear.

I immediately begin to dread the trip. That night in the bedroom, I'm holding you, David, telling you how again and forever I'm scared. You, as is your job these days, comfort and reassure me: "I'll protect you." You make the mistake of saying, "If you don't want to go, you can stay home."

I start in, "You don't want me to go, it will be too hard for you, the workshops are your chance to get away."

"No, no, no. I want you to come. I want to work with you again. You have the special something—the workshops are better with you there."

"I'm in a wheelchair, I'm a freak, everyone will hate me . . ."

This conversation goes on and on and on for the next three

weeks. Every night David says, "Shut up; you're going." Every morning, I tell Teresa I'm not going and every morning she sits by me and tells me the fairy tale of how everyone is making ready the red carpet for the Queen. Deep inside me, I know I'll go.

I list my fears to Gwen:

1. I'm afraid I'll wet myself, or worse yet, crap myself on the plane.
2. I won't have enough energy to do the workshop.
3. Everyone will stare at me.
4. People in the audience will hate me.
5. I'll be a burden forever.

Gwen says, "If you think that's bad—don't worry, I'll have my period, you'll have yours. I'll bleed all over. You'll bleed all over. This will be the first workshop that people hate. Just the everyday things will go wrong so you don't have to worry about anything else."

Gwen can go on like this forever. She makes me laugh and I chime in, "You'll forget to empty my leg bag and it will explode."

"You'll probably fart when David transfers you to the plane seat. The flight attendants will be blown away, and if we take Alan he'll be so annoying on the flight that no one will notice you."

Everything is falling into place. Candice arrives with my beautiful, newly made clothes. A khaki-colored terry-cloth suit for plane travel. A suit of chocolate-brown chintz with military-looking pants and jacket and a fuchsia blouse. A tan linen suit.

We are traveling first class so I can get to my seat in the plane with my wheelchair.

The door to this plane opens in the middle of the plane and I am to sit in the front. The flight attendants bring an aisle chair, and David transfers me and guides me into the plane while the attendant wheels from behind. I am mortified. I feel like baggage. I am ashamed and embarrassed. David is angry; he had taken great pains to ensure my direct transfer from wheelchair to plane. Teresa and Gwen are upset. I want to go home.

Before we land, I put on makeup and comb my hair. No one here is going to know what I'm really like.

※

This time the *front* door opens and after everyone leaves, my wheelchair arrives and the transfer is uneventful. The other David, my cop, greets me with a big kiss and outside, in the airport, we find folks with signs of welcome. I am touched. The van is fine and the room at the hotel is great. They've even managed to get a medical equipment store to rent us a shower chair. The nurse leaves something to be desired. She can't lift or pivot me so David has to transfer me to the toilet, but what the hell . . .

"It's not too bad, is it, PY?" No, I admit grudgingly, not wanting to give up or in yet.

The next day we visit Tulsa—Oral Roberts University and the terrific museum with all the Remingtons and Russells. We are treated so well, with such gracious kindness, that I will always be grateful to the Toughlove people of Tulsa.

Friday night we are lying in bed talking about tomorrow's workshop.

"David, this is better than being home without you."

"I'm so glad you are here with me. It's a lot better than being away by myself."

"Are you sure I'm not too much of a burden?"

"Phyllis, the sharing, being together and getting to work with you again more than makes up for the extra effort. Just look at what we did today. The museum was great. Usually I just hang around the hotel. Your being here makes these workshops a lot more enjoyable for me."

"Are you sure?"

"Yes, my dear, I'm positive."

When we begin the workshop for the one hundred cowboy-type folks that come because their hearts ache to help their children in trouble, they give us a standing ovation. David and I cry. The two-day workshop goes well. I do less than before— any time my leg bag needs emptying, Gwen takes me to my room—but I can still help people. I make the crowd laugh, cry. I can still work an audience.

At the end of the workshop, they honor us even more with a stained-glass engraved Toughlove logo with the date of the workshop on it. My other David says, "You're still the same little gal." We rest for a day and head home. I am okay on the plane. Everyone is pleased and I note that I'm feeling less scared.

At my three-month checkup at Magee, I brag about my trips.

All the nurses pat me on the back and I can feel them feeling proud of me.

They tell me that the old God-calling major in the room next to me died of his bedsores in the nursing home.

XXIX

PHYLLIS

❋ September 4, my birthday, has come. I've screamed and yelled about no celebration but Gwen said, "You haven't got the right to stop my joy." So I keep quiet.

Ilene has come to visit and she tells me "Put on makeup, Ma." I guess that others are coming to celebrate my birthday.

Even so, when I come into the living room I am surprised. My kids and grandchildren along with my friends are here with gifts and cheers to celebrate my life.

We all go outside to the pool where a barbecue and birthday cake are waiting. From the lawn chair David has placed me in I watch people swim and frolic. By six o'clock the kids have cleaned up and everyone has gone home.

"David, it was good, but my real birthday is October eighth," I tell him, referring to the date of the accident.

"This is your birthday!"

On October 8 I wake with dreams of my mother on the edge of my conscious mind and tears on the rims of my eyes.

In my dream my mother calls to me down a long tunnel. She is a twilight shadow standing at a washboard sink. She is silent and sad. "Mama, I beg, please speak to me, hold me."

"Why should I talk, you never heard me," and she is silent again. In the dream I am singing "Sometimes I Feel Like a Motherless Child" a long, long way from home.

David rolls over and holds me while I mourn.

"It's okay, Phyllis, you're making it. I love you," you croon and cry.

"Hold me, David, without you I can't be."

"Now get dressed, we're going to Bloomingdale's." I don't protest. Bloomingdale's is my favorite place.

In Bloomie's the aisles are wide, the floors are not carpeted, so I can wheel myself and the store isn't crowded. I buy Perry Ellis black and brown shoes, new makeup in fallish colors. David gets a new sweater. We eat warm croissants and Godiva chocolates. At home, at night in bed David holds me.

On Christmas Day, I am dressed for the holiday—velvet and white satin, black patent leathers. The girls are busy in the kitchen; the little children—overwhelmed with presents, warm Christmas cheer, chocolate Santas, food smells, adult hustle and bustle—play irritably together. From time to time we say or hear one of us say, "Chris, that's too wild." "Ian, give that to Nitya." "Nitya, stop crying."

Every catalogue has been searched and presents ordered. Nitya's doll carriage, Ian's stuffed animals, Christopher's puppet theater, nightgowns, jewelry, clothes that will be liked and disliked, kept and exchanged—they're all under the tree.

Food is heating—the catered goose, roast beef, plum pudding, potatoes—sweet and mashed, broccoli, acorn squash, cakes, pies—are all ready to eat. Cider, champagne, mulled wine also await us. The table is set with Christmas plates and Santa tablecloths. The Olitskys join us.

I want everything perfect, perfect! More than normal.

Ilene is pouring cider into every glass on the table. "Ilene, stop, don't do that!" I'm screaming. "Not everyone wants cider!"

It's no big thing. "It's easier like this," she says in her I-have-to-much-to-do voice. She's done it—made things easier, not perfect.

"Empty them, put out other cups! I want to fix this right."

Jodi chimes in, "Ma, you're being crazy."

"I'm not. I want it done a certain way," I'm crying.

Heidi: "Okay, okay, stop making a big deal."

Ilene: "How can you talk, Heidi? You didn't do anything!"

"Ilene, you always start. I did a lot. You always think you're better than me."

Everything's ruined. We're having a normal family holiday, not a perfect one. "Go home, all of you," I rant.

Alan steps into the kitchen and takes charge. "Out, Phyllis. Go talk to Gwen," he says. "Heidi, get the food on the table. Jodi, get the kids. Ilene, help Heidi. And all of you apologize." We do, tearfully.

David has been in the bathroom while all this is going on. Typical—definitely not perfect.

In the evening, just before going home, Heidi, Jodi, and Ilene lie on my bed; the kids on the floor. They plead, one at a time, "Next year, just us, no company, not so much food or presents. Please, Ma. Just let's enjoy each other and the kids. The hell with the rest."

I give in. "Okay, 1985 will be simpler." Maybe perfect.

DAVID

✳ Phyllis has pored over at least a million mail order catalogues and we spent several days wheeling through shopping malls. The involvement and pleasure that she gets from all this hustle and bustle always amazes me. She has purchased a seemingly endless array of presents. We ordered dinner from a gourmet take-out restaurant and everything is ready. We are prepared to have a memorable Christmas.

It turned out that everything was not perfect; we even had the usual squabbles. The grandchildren were totally overwhelmed and we put away presents that were opened but unseen for future holidays.

The end of the day left us all exhausted and promising each other, once again, to be sensible next year.

PHYLLIS

※   On a trip to Washington, we stay at the Hilton, where Ilene works. She's proud of the accessibility of the hotel for people like me, which her master's thesis helped evolve. We are proud of her.

I am working all the time now. Radio phone-in shows—it seems I'm doing two or three a week. Toughlove over and over again, blah, blah. Getting up for the shows is tiring. They leave me breathless. My lung capacity is still only 70 percent so talking exhausts me.

Then I work some more, staff meetings, writing a new cocaine manual, then some more resting.

Traveling, doing workshops. In San Antonio, we were met by Toughlove parents, yellow roses, and a mariachi band. I am both mortified and flattered, but also tired.

In Massachusetts, California, and Oregon, we get standing ovations and the sincere thanks of thousands of parents who feel we've saved their lives, their families, their kids. I'm exhausted and worst of all, food has crept back into my life to offer comfort. Food warms and excites me, relieves tiredness, tickles and pleasures my psyche while it destroys my body and pride. I'm fatter.

I'm tired and I have my tenth cold of the year. My physical exhaustion and poor lung capacity make me fair game for every virus around.

Somebody save me!!!

"How can I live like this? It's like I've grown very old all at once. I haven't had the gradual time to get used to legs that swell, ache, and stop moving . . . the time to accept a leaking bladder or incontinent bowel." As I'm saying this I know inside me that what bothers me most is that David does not make love to me. When I ask him he lies, "I'm too busy," or "I thought you were too tired." I feel I am undesirable, and so with this sexlessness goes my youth and his.

I'm tired of bringing up sex so instead I say, "How would you like to learn everything all over again just to live your life in a wheelchair? I don't want to manage anymore."

"You will," you shout, "you will just do it! You will learn. You're worth it. I don't want to be without you."

"You'd be better off without me. You will find someone else who can be a real partner. You don't need this old, flabby body."

"Bullshit."

I am silent.

DAVID

✳ I don't know what to do about sex. I heard a TV talk-show guest say, "Do it or lose it." I worry if I've lost it and that's why I don't feel sexual. I love Phyllis dearly but to me sex seems superfluous.

Somehow I can't get out of my caretaker role to become a lover. Going to bed at night means making sure Phyllis is lying straight so her neck and shoulders won't hurt, and when they hurt I have to massage her. In the morning there are other tasks, more hurts in need of massaging, getting water, wash cloths, clothes, and on and on, endlessly.

When we have time I feel I'm imposing my needs on Phyllis. Instead I work and do the physical tasks of lifting, pushing, and getting that make Phyllis's life possible. I know she wants me to make love to her and instead I do things for her.

To make matters worse, I can't say this because Phyllis will only feel more hurt than she is, and I won't do that to her. Instead I say, "I'm tired," or "You're tired," or "I'm too busy."

PHYLLIS

✳ People who tell me they understand my wanting to

commit suicide are not helpful. They say they have been in bad places too and can understand my desire, but I hear them silently telling me to do it—that I am such a mess I shouldn't want to live. People who tell me to shut up make me angry but at least they don't sanction my death.

On New Year's Day, my new life looms cold, my body is freezing inside and outside.

I am an icy seated statue. My thoughts hold the chill of death. Besides all this, I have a chronic cold and I am fat.

 XXX

DAVID

❊ Each time a workshop is scheduled all of us in the Toughlove office push her to go. Each time Phyllis returns she needs three weeks to recover. I keep hoping she'll recoup faster but it's getting worse. I feel badly, but working gives Phyllis so many goodies: She gets out of herself, she gets great feedback, she's energized, she can see how competent and effective she still is. She finds out that her wheelchair doesn't make her any less of a person.

But the price is high and Phyllis has to pay it. This time she has had enough.

We've returned from one of our many weekend workshops and Phyllis is into her suicide litany.

David, kill me:

I can't stand this life.
It's not worth it.
I'm exhausted.
I'm in such pain.
I want to die.

PHYLLIS

✳ I cannot survive our anniversary and I only want to talk to myself. There is a veil between all of them and me. No more eating or drinking. I get out of bed only for the toilet. One night I reach up for my pills from the bathroom shelf and they fall all over the floor. A few go down my throat. David hears the noise and sees the pills floating in the toilet, on the sink and on the floor. He turns pale and then red. "What the hell are you doing!"

"Leave me alone!"

"I won't," he insists. "Get the hell back in bed!" He throws me into bed.

DAVID

✳ I'm feeling terribly, terribly sad and helpless. I don't know what to do. Intellectually I can say, "Well, it's her life and if it's intolerable she has a right to end it." Emotionally I know I will not let Phyllis leave me. I'm selfish but I can't stand the thought of losing my best friend, my love, and lover all at once. I confide in Nurse Ellen when she comes to help Phyllis shower and get ready for bed. Ellen tells me she will report it to the hospital.

What a dope!

What a jerk!

What the hell is the matter with me! I slipped back into my old routine of thinking I had to do everything myself. That it was up to me to solve Phyllis's suicidal tendencies. Whew! What a relief to recognize what I was doing to myself. I call Teresa, Gwen, and Jodi and we agree that Phyllis will be put in the hospital tomorrow if it is needed.

In the morning we all gather together and tell Phyllis she must start functioning again or it's off to the nuthouse for her. Phyllis is adamant; she doesn't care. She says she is going to kill herself as soon as she can. We make preparations to have her committed to a psychiatric ward. An ambulance will arrive in a couple of hours. I start packing the needed supplies, Jodi packs the clothes, and Gwen and Teresa lie in bed with Phyllis.

Suddenly Phyllis screams at Jodi. "Don't treat my jacket like that. The shirt and pants you just packed don't match. All right! All right, I give up. I won't kill myself now. I'm not going to another hospital ever!"

So Gwen coaxes, "Eat a little eggy, baby, a little cereal. Come, I'll cook," she teases.

I have the solution to suicide: Make a mess out of Phyllis's clothes.

Soon the entire county knows that Phyllis wanted to die. People are calling left and right. So much for confidentiality.

PHYLLIS

✳ "David, I can't keep working all the time. I need time for my body. I'm so tired. My continuous bedsore never heals and it's getting worse."

"It's okay with me," he says easily.

"But, David, you know I hate to exercise and you don't encourage me. Everyone wants me to work, but I can't. I really can't. I'm falling apart. I have no choice." I'm crying again.

"Look, my dear Phyllis, you don't have to convince me," says David the old jock, the workout king.

"I know, but you don't understand. I can't run off to the gym and do my workout. I need help and it means asking you for more, asking Gwen and Teresa for more time away from work. I feel guilty."

"Phyllis, tomorrow we'll hold a support meeting for you. I can call it."

"Will you, David?" I whine.

"I'll be glad to."

DAVID

✳ I ask Gwen, Teresa, and Jodi to come to a meeting with Phyllis and me.

"I've called this meeting because Phyllis and I need your help. We need a support group just like Toughlove. We don't need to do a crisis assessment, we all know what the crisis is. Phyllis can't live the way we have been going. She's working too hard, she's physically exhausted."

Everyone agrees that getting Phyllis working has now become the disease.

"Okay, Phyllis, what's your *stand,* your long-term goal?"

"All I know is I can't work so hard. I have to take care of myself. I feel all of you pressuring me to keep on working."

Both Gwen and Teresa sheepishly agree that they are pressuring her.

"What's your bottom line, Phyllis? What is the first thing you're going to do?" I say, keeping to the task.

"I'm going to call my physical therapist Holly and ask her to set up an exercise and weight program. I'll also call Smith Hospital and find out about their handicap swim program."

"That sounds great, PY. Now, what's your plan and support?"

"I'm going to call as soon as we end this stupid meeting. I just need you guys to stop pushing all this work on me."

A guilty Teresa says, "I won't schedule Phyllis to do any more workshops unless she asks to go."

Gwen says, "I'll monitor the phone calls and Teresa and I will handle what we can and the rest I'll give to David."

"I'll make sure Nitya leaves you alone when you're exercising. I'll also give you massages when your neck and shoulders hurt," comments Jodi.

"I'm going to ask Holly to give me a copy of your exercise regimen so I can help you get it organized," I say. "I'll take you swimming. I'm going to do all the call-in radio shows and finish the rest of the work on our cocaine manual."

"Don't be silly, I can do *some* work, David!"

"Okay, we'll meet next week to see how we're doing."

It's funny. We are these hotshot self-help support people and it takes a suicide attempt to get us to put it to work.

PHYLLIS

✳ At my checkup at Magee, I still will not commit to living, but I do commit to exercise. Dr. Marx gives me a prescription for swimming as he scolds me, "You still have more to do. Do more weight shifts. You need to get rid of your bedsore."

"When will you stop blaming me?" I ask. He laughs. I feel depressed.

The grapevine at Magee informs me that Lady Di has taken a job at Jeff.

I've joined the Smith Hospital disability swim program. They meet at the YMCA. They have a hydraulic lift to get me in and out of the pool, which I hate. Instead David positions my wheelchair at the edge of the pool and slides me out of my chair into a sitting position on the ground. We need to make sure my legs go into the water and don't crumple under me. David then gets behind me and slides me inch by inch into the pool. Getting out is tougher. It takes two people, one under each arm, to lift me up onto the pool edge and then to lift me into my chair.

Before, I'd swim a mile at the Y in about forty-five minutes. Now I need three physical therapists, a life jacket, weights on my waist to keep my head up, and a mask and snorkel to swim two laps in five minutes, and this is nothing compared to getting me showered and dressed afterward. I still love the water and I try. My physical therapist for swimming says I'll learn as I get stronger. I cry.

My balance is so nonexistent that I can't float. I cannot forget my body and I do not forgive it. I can roll myself into bed, leg over leg. But out in the world it's another story. I practice with a transfer board and I'm weight-lifting. All the time I gave to work I now give to my body.

Hal has come with diet tapes and tape recorders. He's lost thirty pounds. I'll try them. He slips me Brucker's number, pats my shoulder, and says, "Call."

"I'm so scared," I say, and he says, "I don't blame you, but call anyway."

Holly has brought me a functional electrical stimulator (FES) to help my breathing and it does. Three months later I have 90 percent of my capacity, up 20 percent and it stays with me with no decrease after I stop using the stimulator. I feel stronger.

And I have found something out. There are actually people out there working on ways to cure spinal cord injury: nerve transplants . . . electrical field to make neurons grow . . . bridging spinal cords.

Magee didn't tell me. "We do not want you to be unrealistic," the doctors, nurses, and social workers say!

Maybe it's all a hoax . . .

DAVID

✳ Phyllis is getting stronger. She has been working out with weights and more exotic paraphernalia. The most obvious change is her breathing. No longer do we have the sudden frightening emergencies of breathlessness caused by an errant crumb or sip of water. Moments when Phyllis would begin frantically waving her arms and pointing, I'd feel I was playing a desperate game of charades. Guess the name of this emergency. When I'd finally understand, we'd do the quadraplegic version of the Heimlich Maneuver: My fist in the solar plexus pushes in when Phyllis exhales; after a few pushes the emergency subsides. The functional electrical stimulation has made the difference. Every night for a month I put the electrodes across her chest and an electrical charge causes her breathing muscles to contract and relax. Her diaphragm is now much stronger and she can actually manage a decent sneeze.

We have a system of rollers that allows Phyllis to sit in place and practice wheeling her chair. She listens to jazz and blues music while pumping away like crazy. The infinitesimal pile on our rugs no longer presents a major obstacle. Phyllis can manage to move around the house on her own, but even better, she can wheel through Bloomingdale's. A reward that has made all the work worthwhile.

"David, do you think I should take driving lessons? Magee and Holly are telling me it will make me more independent. You know I always hated driving. I'm always getting lost."

"You might as well learn how to drive. I'm sure the hand control of the disability cars' speed and brakes is different. Maybe you'll like it. If you still hate it you don't have to do it."

We meet the driving instructor in a large shopping mall parking lot. Phyllis needs to be transferred by wheelchair from our car to the hand-controlled instructor's car. I wait in our car until they return. Their departure is a little erratic, the car lurches and weaves. But after all, this is Phyllis's first try.

On our way home after the lesson I ask Phyllis how it went.

"I was so nervous I kept talking and didn't pay attention. When he told me to turn left I went right, if he said right I went left."

I laughed, "So what's new about that? Sounds to me like your usual driving."

"The instructor asked me if I was sure I wanted to drive. I told him no and he said that's good because you're not good at it."

"That's pretty straightforward. Are you going to try again?"

"Yeah, I figured I'll give it one more try. I have an appointment at the same time and place next week."

Next week we meet and I put Phyllis in her wheelchair to move her the five feet between our cars. I don't bother with the removable footrest but pick up Phyllis's legs to propel her. No sooner have we started than the chair tilts over backward and Phyllis smacks her head on the macadam.

"Oh, my God, what's wrong with me?" and I'm sitting next to you holding you in my arms. Your arms are around me and we are both crying.

"How are you, Phyllis?"

"Oh, David, my head aches and my hands and neck are numb, but I'm okay." She pats me to comfort me.

After what seems like an eternity her hands, arms, and neck stop tingling. The driving instructor and I get Phyllis in our car. He asks, "Are you okay, Phyllis?"

"I don't want to drive. I hate it. My goal is to get a chauffeur some day."

All I can say on the way home is, "Jesus, how could I do this to you? I'm so dumb."

"David stop! It was my responsibility too. You know I don't want to drive. Do you mind? I can't get in and out of the car anyway."

"I'm relieved." Phyllis has a terrible headache and a large lump as a souvenir of my carelessness.

When we tell Teresa, Gwen, and Jodi about your giving up driving they're happy you won't be a danger to them on the road anymore.

XXXI

DAVID

❋ We've come to California to be on the set of *Toughlove,* the film. While we are here we check out a rehabilitation clinic that claims to get every injured person walking.

I'm always cynical about claims to make our bodies work better. Taking large doses of megavitamins, eating a diet of vegetables, fruit, macrobiotics, microbiotics, Pritikin, jogging, swimming, lecithin, meditating, and all the other programs. Spinal cord injury and its gurus of care are no exception. The motivation here is greater. We are shown around and see an intensive physical therapy program consisting mostly of weight-lifting.

The climax of our visit is to see a young man, with an injury just below the level of Phyllis's injury, walk. The thin, intense-looking man is buckled into braces that leave him looking like a plastic Sir Galahad. With one attendant in front and one attendant behind, he is helped to stand and hold on to the parallel bars. His arms vibrate fiercely, but he stands by himself. He inches along on the bar and with each forward hand movement he swings his shoulder which propels his leg under him. By alternating back and forth, the perspiring, straining, heroic young man "walks" five feet. Phyllis and I applaud as his armor is removed and he returns exhausted to his wheelchair. In talking to him we discover that he works out eight hours a day six days a week. Phyllis and I are crestfallen. We are both too old for the regimen of an Olympic athlete. We want more in our life than exercise. Phyllis's aesthetic sensibilities cause her to shudder at the thought of her body encased in plastic.

PHYLLIS

✳ We are on the set, a home in Brentwood, California, which is dressed up to be Anywhere, USA by scattering eastern pine trees around the lawn and dressing actors in fall clothes. We're playing at playing extras, it's exciting. After four long years of ups and downs, good scripts and bad, rejections from networks and cable companies, Toughlove is going to be seen by millions of people in ordinary homes; it will run this fall on the Sunday night ABC Movie of the Week.

Stars and extras are working hard, waiting in the hot sun for their call. For us, this is an extraordinary experience.

Lee Remick is lovely, gracious, bright, and charming. Bruce Dern is funny and has more of a motor mouth than I have.

TV Guide, the *Los Angeles Times,* and *Entertainment Tonight* interviews have us "up and on." We love our ten minutes of fame, glamour, and glitz.

From our film debut we take off to Alaska for a one-day workshop and vacation.

Alaskan parents struggling with kids running wild and stomping out life are the same desperate, pained parents seeking help that we see everywhere. We *do* help!

Alaska is different from other places we have been to in the

United States. Even Anchorage has a quality of an old Western town, perhaps right out of an old Western movie. A little muddy-looking; an old cemetery with whalebone headstones in the middle of town; flat low buildings; the tall buildings are dwarfed by the surrounding mountains and by comparison with buildings in other cities I've seen. There are a few log cabins still in sight, folks wearing cowboy boots or high-top work shoes hanging out in not-so-savory places. Eskimos burdened by poverty, the kind of drunken poverty that encrusts the eye lids, cracks the skin, and gives babies respiratory infections. The kind we pretend we don't have, the kind that makes me feel I should do something. Instead I look away toward the "purple mountains' majesty." We drive the Alaskan Highway, past white foxes walking railroad tracks that run next to the sea. There are snow-covered volcanoes and teal-green mountain lakes. Moose meander across the road, and most surprising is the Windex-window-clean blue of the glaciers. Icy blue.

Fishermen are everywhere, and all we do is eat. We enjoy wonderful fresh halibut and salmon: We eat them broiled, boiled, dried, fried, baked, poached, and salted. Pickled salmon delights our palates.

Senses satiated, egos stroked, we're feeling good as we head home.

In Chicago we miss our plane and our luggage leaves for Philadelphia. We're stranded at ten o'clock at night with no medical supplies except an extra small leg bag and we're frantic. We find a hotel with an inaccessible bathroom but we manage anyway.

David schlepps me on and off the toilet and into bed. We put the two leg bags together to collect my urine during the night. Hooray for us. We made it but from now on I'll be prepared.

At home I pack an emergency kit in my wheelchair backpack that will stay with me all the time. My kit includes:

large overnight leg bag
small daytime leg bag
extra leg straps to hold the leg bags on
rubber gloves to cover the finger that opens the sphincter
lubricating jelly for my finger
alcohol swabs to clean up urine spills

needleless hypodermic to fill the balloon in my catheter
extra catheter
diaper, just in case
clean panties, because I like to be clean
toothbrush and toothpaste
tampon

DAVID

✳   Our travel experiences have taught us the meaning of "buyer beware." We carefully check out our seats on airlines now to make sure Phyllis is not stashed in the middle row of seats that I can't possibly get her into. We make reservations at hotels that guarantee us that we have a wheelchair-accessible room. Even so, we frequently find things are not as promised. So at hotels, Phyllis waits in the cab in case we need to find another place to stay.

In a Pasadena, California, hotel the guaranteed accessible room has a bathroom with no door. I am furious. "How many other guests are paying for a room without a bathroom door?" I demand to know. "We are bringing one hundred and ninety people into your hotel for a weekend workshop. And we can't have a room with a bathroom door?"

The desk clerk is very sorry, "But we have no other accommodations."

The assistant manager says, "We always rent rooms with the bathroom door off to handicapped people. No one's complained before."

The manager says, "I'm terribly sorry, what do you want us to do?"

By now I've retreated to the old assertiveness technique: "You have a problem. How do you intend to solve it?" Inside me I'm furious and I strain to appear calm. I also refuse to go back to *their* office and insist on carrying on this loud discussion in the lobby.

After a hot, heavy, and angry hour we are given a suite. A bedroom with a bathroom door off and a living room and guest bathroom with a door on. I go and collect Phyllis from the cab.

PHYLLIS

✳ All week long I'm fuming, I'm hot, and I'm mad about our "guaranteed accessible hotel." Finally I make a decision and I call the hotel manager. "I want to do you a favor and offer you the chance for some training in accessibility and disability on Tuesday afternoon at 3 P.M." And I quietly add, "Or you can have a civil suit brought against you."

At 3 P.M. we have four wheelchairs ready for their top management people. We ask the banquet manager to sit in the corner and not move no matter what. We tie a person's legs to the foot of the bed and ask him to operate the TV across the room or answer the out-of-reach phone. We put a person into a wheelchair and inform him not to move from the waist down. He has five minutes to get onto the toilet or he will soil himself. He quickly gets into the doorless bathroom and finds he has only enough room to face the toilet head-on. He cannot manage the task in time. A woman friend of ours, playing chambermaid, knocks and enters the room, catching him in the bathroom. I quietly say, "Don't answer, but how do you feel?"

David takes four people in wheelchairs to their "accessible" restaurant that requires a three-stair lift. The rugs in the halls are so thick that even the able-bodied have a hard time wheeling. The elevator doors close so quickly that the assistant manager asks, "How do we get into the elevator?"

"It's a problem, isn't it?"

At the restaurant, helpers drop a person out of the chair because they lift incorrectly. Back in the room, the banquet manager tearfully asks, "Why have you left me here? What have I done?"

"You are in the same position I am in as a guest in your hotel."

Some of the staff want to engage in an intellectual discussion: "What are the building codes?"

"What changes can we make?"

In my best firm voice I slowly and clearly enunciate, "You can find out about building codes elsewhere. What I want you to know is how mean, thoughtless, and inconsiderate you are to me, a guest in your hotel."

Still someone pipes up and says, "Yes, but how can we make this hotel more accessible?"

With calculated murder in my eyes I carefully address her. "Listen, my dear, you are never to tell people that this hotel is accessible! But I really want *you* to know how cruelly and carelessly you have treated and are treating me."

Only the general manager and the banquet manager come up and say, "I'm sorry." The rest file out looking shaken or indignant.

Two weeks later I call the hotel and ask if they have wheelchair-accessible rooms. The front desk clerk assures me they are not accessible.

Tonight we are in Detroit on Dennis Wholey's *Late Night America* TV show, telling the late-night world how this injury has affected our life.

"How's it going, Phyllis?" Dennis already knows the trouble we've had just getting to the show.

"You really want to know? Well, for openers, the airline promised us a jetway in Detroit and there was none. I got carried off with the help of cops, swearing and, if I could've, kicking all the way, down the plane steps and up two flights to the airport. Next, the lovely hotel that is building accessible rooms which aren't quite ready lied to us and gave us the runaround."

"Where are you staying?"

David speaks up, "At the Blanding Hotel on an unfinished floor in an unfinished room."

"The insurance company spent two hundred thousand dollars to keep me alive and I can barely find places to go or be. You know, Dennis, sometimes I even forget I am in a wheelchair but this inaccessible world reminds me. It's not the wheelchair that's awful; it's being different and left out. I am married to my wheelchair and like all newlyweds I feel a certain ambivalence. I dislike the limits and boundaries of this relationship but I value the freedom I have within its confines.

"I am wheelchair-mobile. What an awkward, unsatisfactory phrase. This state of being has no satisfactory image, no comfortable language. We talk of disabled, abnormal, physically challenged, handicapped, crippled because we are not satisfactory, typical, or of normal design. We cannot situate ourselves in the world, a world designed for walkies, seeies, hearies. As long as ramps, wide doorways, wheelchairs are seen as an *extra,* a *special,* so we'll be seen as extraordinary.

"I feel that people who are disabled are presented to the public like objects of pity or show dogs that can do tricks. The best, most difficult trick gets the most applause or money for charity. Can a wheelchair athlete just be an athlete? Can a deaf actress just be an actress? Can I just be a writer—well, a good writer?"

The speech falls out of my mouth. I didn't even know it was in there. Dennis asks what happened after the accident and David speaks of our long months of separation and pain. We cry. We laugh. "I love you, dearest," I say for the whole world to hear.

The switchboard is lighting up. Empathy pours in, people relate.

When we get home, letters come. Some people think we'll make fine representatives for the disability community.

At home again, I am awake and thoughts of the early days of my injury are in my head. "David, wake up!" As usual, he is alert to me.

"What's wrong?"

"Nothing. I want to know if a support person or group would have been helpful to you from the first day on?"

"Don't scare me or wake me again like that! Goodnight, and I think so!"

My head is running a mile a minute, spelling out the hand-holding, the questions to answer, the follow-through out in the community. A family-support network lives.

A week later, David and I present Jefferson and Magee with our idea for a "Family Spinal Cord Network," a telecommunications conference for all the national spinal cord centers, presenting a family model from day of injury right to coming home. We'll work at it. They are supportive.

After the meeting I stop to see Lady Di outside the intensive care unit.

"Phyllis, we're getting married." She's happy and seems serious about her life. I'm glad. For the first time I look at the ICU and see the womb from which I came. I think to myself, "It's okay that I am alive."

XXXII

DAVID

❋ The Toughlove movie is a smash, winning top ratings of the evening. Fifty million families watched, enthralled. Our office phones are ringing off the hook night and day. Reports about rotten kids, overflowing group meetings, Toughlove open houses from Iowa to Maine and from Los Angeles to Alaska reach us. Even *we* loved the movie. We're a smash. But, where are our film debuts? Alas, on the cutting-room floor.

Good-bye Hollywood.

Hello three hundred new groups.

PHYLLIS

❋ Holly, my physical therapist, has come to measure me

for a new wheelchair. "Phyllis, have you heard of a Dr. Brucker from Miami?"

"Yes, my friend Hal has mentioned him a lot. He keeps trying to get me to go and see him. I asked Dr. Marx about Brucker and he told me that my injury is complete and biofeedback will only work with incomplete injuries."

"I went to a conference on spinal cord injury last week and I heard Dr. Brucker talk. He doesn't believe in an injury to the spinal cord being complete unless the cord is totally severed. He thinks you get return of function all your life. In half an hour he can test you on a biofeedback device he has invented to see if you have any nerve-muscle pathways working below the level of injury."

"I don't know, Holly. I keep reading about people making great claims, but most of them turn out to be extensive physical therapy programs."

"I saw a tape of his work and it's really impressive. I think I'd like to go to Miami and study with him."

"Do you think I should see him?"

"Why not? You've nothing to lose."

Later I tell David what Holly said and ask him, "Should I go and see Dr. Brucker?"

"I don't know. I'm afraid."

"Me too."

DAVID

❋ "Phyllis, I've just read an article by a sex therapist who is using biofeedback on vaginal muscles to enhance bladder control."

"I wonder if it would help me? I'd give anything to get rid of this leg bag."

"I don't know if it would help or not. He lives close by, should I give him a call?"

"Sure, why not."

The therapist arrives with a plastic dildo that is connected to a biofeedback machine. When pressure is put on the dildo the screen records the amount of the response. We spend an hour each night practicing. The screen records numbers that seem to have no rhyme or reason. Whatever pressure is being recorded has no relationship to Phyllis. Our sex life improves but Phyllis's bladder refuses to be aroused.

PHYLLIS

※ I am horny a lot—at the same old times as always, before my period and after it. It's so easy now to see the biology of me.

The horniness is in the lower part of my abdomen, above the pubis, and in my vagina. Massaging that part of the stomach feels great, but no cigar. I resent having no orgasm. I suppose I should be happy with good feelings, but I'm not! After sex, I cry. I think it's a release for me.

We have a few positions that allow David to stay inside. "Phyllis, roll over." David positions my legs and puts himself in dog-style. His penis feels better in me than before. It's as if I can still feel inside pleasure now that I've lost outside sensation. His thrust and increasing hardness help to massage the horny spot and I feel good.

I try my best to be good in bed. I give him oral sex. This pleases David, but is not his favorite. Unfortunately, the old in-and-out is. I try hard to move.

Aunt Beaty called from Florida this morning to tell me that she saw a doctor on TV who is working with spinal cord injury people making muscles work. She stopped to call Uncle Harry. "Come here, Harry, get me that piece of paper with the doctor's name on it for Phyllis," she directs in her army general tone that I have inherited; and they start to shout, "Where did you put it Beaty?" "Over by the sink. Look, open your eyes." "Oyee, I found it!" "Right under his nose," she says into the phone and I can hear my uncle say, "You're a pain in the behind." My aunt laughs.

"Dr. Bernard Brucker is the name. He's doing something with spinal cords at the University of Miami. Go, darling, go find out. Maybe it's something." And she means, maybe I'll walk.

"Thanks, Aunty."

The *Paraplegia News* has come and the pages are filled with articles by and about Bernard Brucker and biofeedback.

Help! Help! I'm surrounded.

I'm afraid, afraid to hope.

Hal is calling me from Florida where he's studying the work that Brucker is doing.

"Phyllis, I'll make you an appointment."

"Okay, Hal." In two weeks I'm going to Miami.

What if he says I'm hopeless? What if . . . no matter what he says I'll want to walk. It will never be good enough! David says, "I know, my darling, but we have to try." You are a pessimistic optimist.

I fear total despair and helplessness will overwhelm me if Brucker can't work with me. I don't want to have to kill myself.

Finally, taking our hearts in our hands we go to Miami to meet our new guru, Dr. Bernard Brucker.

The hospital is crowded with many people of different colors. The crippled children hanging out around the place hurt me most of all. I look at everyone, trying to pick out quads from paras. David and I find Dr. Brucker's lab and wait outside his door.

Black hair, black beard, dark-skinned hairy hands, sexy, alive, seductive, Bernard Brucker makes me feel good in a minute. So positive. His eyes light up when I say my injury was at 6–7 cervical.

"My God, I'm so excited. You're so incomplete. You've gotten so much return. You'll get more. Let's see, let's see." He talks about return as he hooks me up to his electrodes, computers, printouts, dials, switches, and buttons, but he never wheels out a Frankenstein monster, and electric bolts of lightning do not flash around the room. Instead I bend over to see if my back muscles are firing neurons, which means I have regenerating connections from my brain to my behind. I'm firing neurons and Dr. Brucker is cheering me on. His excitement is contagious for David and me. David is cheering me on. I am amazed at David's joy, that he loves me so much, that my life is so important to him.

On the phone that night, we share our joy with Hal. He acts as though he'd known it all along. Teresa, Gwen, Jodi, Ilene, Heidi,

Dale, Mary, and all the others are happy and I don't have to kill myself.

DAVID

❋ Being with Dr. Brucker is like mainlining enthusiasm. He believes in life and nerve regeneration after spinal cord injury and in a few seconds he's made believers of Phyllis and me. He has refused to accept the death knell of spinal cord injury: "Your injury is complete. You can only strengthen what you have. You will never get more muscle function." He has designed a system of electrodes that are taped to useless muscles and has attached these to a computer. He then manually moves the hand, arm, torso, leg and asks the injured person to try and help. The electrodes pick up the minuscule electrical charges of nerves firing and show them on a computer screen. If Dr. Brucker does all the work, nothing happens. If the patient does some of the work, the screen will show how much.

The minute we step into his laboratory he tells Phyllis that she has an incomplete injury and hurriedly puts his electrodes on muscles in her lower back. Phyllis lowers her chest to her knees and Dr. Brucker pushes her up saying, "Come on, push, you can do it. Wow! look at the screen! Look at what your muscles are doing!" The line has gone to the top of the graph and leveled off. "That was four percent! Look at that! I can't believe it! You have so much return."

He ups the graph to 16 percent and we try again. I'm so excited I'm shouting now, "Come on, Phyllis, you can do it. Make that line travel. Hit the top of the graph. Come on." The line squiggles between 10 and 12 percent. We keep trying until Phyllis starts to lose it. Dr. Brucker stops. Phyllis is fatigued but happy. My skepticism returns.

"How do you explain what's happening?" I ask.

"I believe spinal nerves regenerate all our life. They just regenerate very slowly. I also believe we have other nerve paths to muscles that we have never learned to use. By showing you that nerves are working on a screen in front of you, your body learns how to use these new pathways. You could see it yourself. As Phyllis learned to use her back muscles, the screen showed it."

At last, a guru I believe in. Phyllis and I are sold.

Dr. Brucker schedules us for an hour appointment every other day for the next two weeks.

Miami seems bigger and brighter than life. The excitement of Dr. Brucker's biofeedback carries over onto everything. Even the warm weather agrees with Phyllis. Best of all, there is a shopping mall nearby with a lot of shoe stores. Phyllis believes she has moved close to heaven.

For the next two weeks we travel to Mecca. Phyllis inches her performance slowly upward. Dr. Brucker tries moving the electrodes lower down on Phyllis's back but very little shows on the graph.

PHYLLIS

✳ For two weeks dear Bernard yells and cheers and encourages me to learn to fire more and more neurons to my immobile back muscles. He's halfway down my back and I'm firing 30 percent of my neurons. Before it's time for me to go home and practice, I force him to test my legs. He warns me, "I don't think there's anything yet," and there's not. "Wishes don't make dreams come true," he tells me in a kindly way.

The day before we leave Miami, Brucker remembers something to tell us. "Do you know about the Miami Project to Cure Spinal Cord Injury?" No, I am skeptical and excited. "And have you met Barth Green? He's head of neurosurgery and the Miami Project. We're gathering the best scientists from all over the world. We want people from any discipline that combines rehabilitation, basic sciences, and clinical, human application of research to spinal cord injury. We are determined to duplicate the same kind of excitement, dedication, brilliance, and energy that created the atomic bomb in the Manhattan Project. The model we're exploring now is the same one they're using for Parkinson's disease. They are experimenting with fetal tissue transplants."

DAVID

✳ Dr. Brucker questions us carefully about Phyllis's injury. "How did it happen? Did you tumble or was it a straight fall?" He wants to know in case Phyllis may have had another break lower down her spine.

"Sometimes hospitals only treat the higher injury and never check to see if there is more than one break. I'm going to ask Dr. Barth Green to look at you."

Barth Green is a small, slim, stiff-spined, pigeon-toed bolt of lightning.

He sends us to magnetic resonance imaging (MRI). Here we see a huge magnet that can show soft tissue just as an x ray shows bones. I sit and watch as the pictures occur. All of Phyllis's inner workings are exposed before my very eyes. I can see a dark line where scar tissue has formed at the injury site. Only one break is in evidence.

Dr. Green suggests and we insist on trying to see if Phyllis can use functional electrical stimulation to ride an exercise bike. Phyllis sits while electrodes are placed on her quadriceps. Electricity goes into her leg muscles which contract and make her leg move. If the electricity can make Phyllis's leg muscles work, she can learn to ride a bike and get the aerobic exercise she needs. Our hope and enthusiasm skyrocket.

PHYLLIS

✳ Dr. Green tells me, "You have to go into our F.E.S. Project. You'll feel better. You'll be healthier and get thinner. He runs with us to the F.E.S. Spinal Cord Lab, asks Mark Nash, the director of the lab, to test my quadricep muscles. Electrodes make the quads contract and I have to leave for the airport. "We can try you on the bike," Mark says. Barth runs out to the car with us, kisses us good-bye, repeating "Call me tonight" as he gives his home number. We make the plane only because it's delayed.

That night from home, we talk; he says, "Make an appointment for the bike," and I tell him about the plan for a Family Spinal Cord Network. He likes it and we send him the proposal and our Toughlove books. The next week he passes it on to the National Spinal Cord Injury Association and they like it.

——— ✳ XXXIII ✳ ———

PHYLLIS

✳   Poor Toughlove waits while I try to mobilize the disability community in my area.

The first meetings are a mess. Never mind our disabilities, but the helplessness, the neediness, the different agendas make our meetings like the Tower of Babel.

DAVID

✳   We meet in the basement of a church. They have made the space accessible for wheelchairs as a service to their handicapped congregation. Unfortunately, for our first meeting the pastor has forgotten to leave the key with anyone and has gone away for the day. We frantically call church members until we locate a key. Meanwhile the sidewalk is crowded with seven people in chairs all lined up in single file while five walkies, one of whom is using crutches, shuttle back and forth letting everyone know what is happening. One of the walkies is our friend Mary who has joined us to help form the support group we hope to create.

Fred and Sue from our couples' group at Magee arrive. Fred doesn't look well. Sue drops Fred off, comes over to say hello and leaves. I ask Fred, "How are you doing?"

"I'm okay."

"You look like you've been ill. Have you been sick?"

"No, Sue and I are not getting along and I'm kinda' upset."

"Yeah, I figured things were not going well when she left so quickly."

"We're getting a divorce. My business is down the tubes and I'm going on Social Security. Sue's had it. She can't stand me. We'll sell the house and I'll move in with my brother until I can think of something else."

"Fred, do you know about attendant care services? The state will help you get an attendant or you can use your own. You pay what you can afford and they pay the rest. You can get help for up to eight hours a day."

"I don't know anything about it. Do you have a number where I can find out about it?"

"I don't have it here with me but give me a call and I'll give it to you." I feel badly for Fred. I guess their rosy outlook when we saw them at Magee didn't last. I wonder what happened.

Finally the key arrives and we file into the meeting room. We form a big circle and introduce ourselves. Phyllis and I explain that we would like to start a spinal cord support group for the injured persons and their families and friends. "I would have liked it if a family member of an injured person could have met me when Phyllis was in intensive care, not to do anything but reassure me. During this time I met some folks who had traveled from three hundred miles away. Their son had been flown by helicopter to Jefferson and they wanted to be by his side. They had no idea of where to go in Philadelphia. It would be really helpful if someone would help folks like this find a place to stay and give them some advice about where to eat and so on."

────────────── ❊

"It would have been helpful if Magee had had a patient welcoming committee," Phyllis says. "I needed some help in learning where different places were. I don't have trouble talking and meeting people but I do know other people are shy. We started a welcome program while I was in Magee but it died when Prince Valiant and I left. I think this is something we can do for others."

We go on talking about the help we could have used at all the juncture points of treatment and especially when we got home. We explain how injured people and their families who are further down the path of recovery could help those just beginning the journey. We ask the other people what they would like to use these meetings for.

Karl, the walkie on crutches says, "I have a degenerative disease. I'll be in a wheelchair in another year and I want to start a chapter of the National Spinal Cord Association here."

Joe, a paraplegic, works for SEPTA, the public transportation system, and he would like to see about getting better public transportation for the handicapped.

Jack, a quad, wants help with his finances. Janis, who is in a wheelchair from a severe case of cerebral palsy, needs a ramp at the entrance of her apartment building. The families are feeling devastated and disjointed. Marriages are disintegrating, parents are feeling helpless before the demands of injured children.

We arrange to meet the following week to see if we can begin to set a direction we can all agree upon.

Going home, Phyllis, Mary, and I are discouraged. Mary counsels us both to have patience. "It's going to take time. Everyone has different needs. If we keep going we should be able to get a core group of people who want to work."

PHYLLIS

❊ For us this group is a reality exploration into the disability community.

As I sit at our meeting in this little church I think about the hours and hours of work I have done calling and researching each organization and its goals. I've ordered all kinds of information, bought books on travel, and I read and read the disability literature, especially those anthologies written by women. I've ordered every magazine I can get hold of that deals with disability.

I have learned that the disability community does not really exist. People are extremely varied. There are so many issues: cure, care, transportation, recreation, accessibility, education, attendant care, family support. The organizations are so many— NOD, NRA, SCS, NSEA, and on and on. The magazines, the newsletters, *Paraplegia News, Disability Rag, Ability, Mainstream Access,* and many more.[1]

All this makes my head swim and I feel I want to unite "my people." I will become the Martin Luther King of disability, in my wheelchair, leading a wheel-in on the runways of the first airline to refuse access to disabled people.

"Let my people go . . ."

Our second meeting is more of the same with almost all new people.

Tyrone, a para, speaks out, "I want to start a Spinal Cord Society chapter. I think we need more research to find a cure. Do you want to stay paralyzed all your life?"

Margaret, who was disabled by polio when she was three, retorts, "Look, I have been disabled all of my life. My home, my job, my relationships, my prejudices, my values, and my pride are all involved with my disability. I'm not sure I want the promised cure. I like my life." And the meeting disintegrates into a cure-versus-care debate.

We leave the meeting promising to meet again in a month. We need some time to plan a better way of running these meetings.

On the way home Phyllis tells me, "You know, David, I just realized that I only imagine that I remember what it is like to walk. But the people who are born with a disability can never miss the physical feeling, knowledge, or ease of being able to hear, see, or walk. In fact, if they gained these things they would

---

[1]For all the information about spinal cord surgery you ever wanted to know, see *Spinal Network,* Sam Maddox, P.O. Box 4162, Spinal Network and Sam Maddox, Boulder, Colorado 80306.

lose their adjustment to the world just as I lost mine when I became disabled."

Three-year-old Nitya, who is growing up, wants to know when I will walk the way she does. We explain that I won't. She says, "You're little because you're in a wheelchair, Grandma."

I draw a diagram for eleven-year-old Christopher of all the connections from my neck to my legs that were crushed by my fall.

Ian, a worried four-year-old, asks who helps me in and out of the car when Grandpa isn't home. "Jodi and other big people."

They all look at the scar on my neck. Christopher even shows his best friend. "And, don't you write books and go on TV and weren't you on Donahue?"

"Yes, it's all true."

"See, I told you so," Christopher says to his friend. No idle boaster he. I'm famous for everything.

The psychologist at Magee invites us to talk to their new couples' group. At the couples' meeting we try to comfort the newly injured and their loves. We laugh, cry, answer questions.

David says, "When we first got hurt, I would have liked to talk to more spouses to see how they were managing. I would have liked to visit other injured people in their homes to see how they lived. When Phyllis left Magee we bought so many extra supplies and medicine that Phyllis never even took. It would have been good to hear someone caution us, 'Go easy on everything. You may not need them very long. You can never tell how quickly you will adjust physically.' Or, 'Phyllis isn't strong enough to haul around all day. Take it easy until you see how her energy level is.' I needed to keep hearing that it takes about two years for the body to adjust to this injury. Don't give up no matter how hard it is in the beginning, it gets better!"

Phyllis tells them, "I like to be with other injured people. It's lonely being the only one around who's short. I like to talk, to find out what other people know. I'm sure we could have made fewer mistakes."

We share with them our idea of a family spinal cord support network. We would like to see the hospital help us train some people to contact and visit with family members. We think these visits should be made once in acute care and again later when the injured person goes into rehab. We'd like to see people exchange phone numbers and commit themselves to making at least one phone call a week to people who have just come home and help them with the adjustments, pain, and everyday realities. We'd like to see the hospital hold one family night each month.

The injured people listen to us, but it is the spouses who are enthusiastic about our ideas. Claude, the spouse of Sylvia who is a para, asks if he can call us when they get home.

"Of course."

I meet Dr. Marx in the hall. "I want to show you how I bend over and get up."

"Okay," he says.

I bend over and get up.

"Oh, you've learned to use spasms."

"No," David says, "it's biofeedback."

"It's my new muscles, back muscles," I protest. Even my physical therapist can see me move my stomach.

"You have learned to compensate—all people do. I am glad you are better and living a good life." And he's off.

I'm so mad, I'm crying, "Closed-minded bastard."

"He's wrong, forget him." David pats my shoulder as we leave. I'm cold. My life is gray for three days—could he be right? I don't even have spasms and still I'm questioning me.

My heart is in Miami. Teresa, Gwen, Mary, and David say "go."

Dale who can stand-pivot me takes me out to dinner before I leave for Miami. In the restaurant she notices that people look away from the wheelchair or get startled when I come up behind them and they haven't seen me. "You know, Phyllis, once I was at an amusement park where I saw a group of disabled vets. They were legless, armless, on crutches, or in wheelchairs. I can remember feeling angry because seeing them spoiled my good time. I felt sadness, pity, fear, and disgust and these feelings lessened my happiness. Why the hell do they have to be here, I thought."

Her honesty makes both of us very sad.

Our last workshop is on June 21. From there, I leave with David for three months' training at the University of Miami.

I leave everyone to work on energizing plans to change our

Toughlove business structure, to do training and workshops, and to take care of everyday business and fill in for me. Everyone sacrifices.

A friend gives us her wonderful Miami condo apartment that's like a movie set to stay in. David, Jodi, Nitya, and Meredith, who has come to be my assistant, will alternate staying there with me. Good-bye Heidi, Ilene, Gwen, Mary, Teresa, and all.

——— * XXXIV * ———

DAVID

* The functional electrical stimulation lab is in the Parkinson Pavilion. As we wheel through the hall we pass elderly people struggling to control bodies that no longer respond well. We smile and pass pleasantries, recognizing our mutual personhood in disability.

The lab is a large room containing four electrical stimulation bikes. Each one has an armchair facing a small computer screen with bicycle pedals attached to a large wheel. People in wheelchairs are waiting for their turn on the bikes, or are just finishing up and hanging around; some are using the hand ergometer, a bicycle-like pedal arrangement that you push by hand against resistance, to increase your aerobic capacity. There are some who sit in their electric-powered chairs with very little hand or arm function but they too can ride the bike. Excitement and camaraderie fill the room.

I will stay in Miami for three weeks; then Jodi and Nitya will come for two weeks and Meredith for two weeks. After this we will rotate on a two-week schedule until Phyllis can ride the bike on her own. We have three days a week in electrical stimulation and two days a week with Dr. Brucker.

Phyllis needs to build up her leg strength before she will be able to ride the bike. Every other day electrodes are placed on her legs, and weights are Velcroed to her ankles. The electrical stimulus is applied and her leg muscles contract to lift the weights. A computer measures how fast she lifts and how much electricity is needed to make the muscles work. If her legs work too slowly or if she needs too much electricity, the computer registers muscle fatigue and stops working. Phyllis needs to lift fifteen pounds ten times in a row before she will be ready to ride the bike. It's a tough job and her muscles respond slowly. Dr. Mark Nash, head of the lab, calls us into his office for a conference. "Phyllis, I'm concerned with the slow progress you're making. We have never worked with a woman your age before and perhaps your age and the excess adipose tissue you have won't let the stimulus work."

With her eyes flashing and nostrils flaring, Phyllis says, "So! I'm doing it anyway." And wheels out of his office and over to the hand ergometer to vent her feelings.

Michael, who is forty and in the functional electrical stimulation program, has been injured for fifteen years. He was in a car accident, got out of the car and walked two miles before collapsing—never to walk again. He has the wisdom and cynicism of the old-time injured. He's not sure he believes in the magic of exercise but he's willing to try. We become friendly with him and his wife Joyce.

He sees Phyllis pumping away and comes over to see what has created such zest. "Hey, Phyllis, if you keep that up you'll become a national bicycle champ."

"I'm really pissed. Nash just told me I'm too fat and too old."

"What did he have in mind?"

Laughter fills our hearts and we plan to go and eat at Wolfie's.

PHYLLIS

❋ Wolfie's is filled with old men coming in for early-bird specials, looking for restaurants with familiar foods like pastrami, boiled chicken, kosher pickles, matzoh balls, plenty of freebies, bread and fruit to take home, salads on the tables, cole slaw, cucumbers, green tomatoes, and all at 1953 prices to brag to friends about.

We sit next to old women discussing their illnesses, medications, canes, walkers, pains, aches, doctors they've tried, and their special diets as they eat everything in sight. In our wheelchairs Michael and I blend right in.

DAVID

❋ Three weeks have flown by so fast I scarcely know where they've gone. I meet Jodi and Nitya at the airport late in the afternoon and take off for home early the next morning. I feel depressed at leaving Phyllis and the excitement of Miami behind.

I've returned just in time to attend our fledgling spinal cord support group. The meeting is a repeat of our previous attempts. Mary, who is there with me, is as discouraged as I am. We don't know how to get past the difficulties of constantly starting over, so we tell people we'll notify them if we decide to meet again.

Two weeks later I get a call from Claude, a spouse from the couples' group Phyllis and I were asked to speak to at Magee. "David, Sylvia's been home for two weeks now. She's constantly depressed and I feel like everything I try to do is wrong. Have you any suggestions?"

"Why don't you do what we ask our Toughlove people to do, call all of your friends and relatives and invite them to your house. Phyllis is in Miami so I'll bring my friend Mary and a couple of people in wheelchairs and we'll plan how we can set up a support system for both of you. Can you do that?"

"Yeah, a bunch of friends of ours have been asking if they could help but Sylvia keeps pushing them away."

"Invite them anyway and we'll just deal with Sylvia when we meet."

"Okay."

Ten of Claude and Sylvia's friends arrive and I bring Mary, Deana, a longtime quad, Victor, a para who knew Sylvia at Magee, and Holly, Sylvia's physical therapist. Sylvia is quiet and forlorn-looking. All the friends say, "We love you. We want to help."

"But, you don't understand. You can't know what it is like." Deana says, "I know what it's like, Sylvia. When I came home I wouldn't face anybody. All I could think about was my fear of losing bladder or bowel control in front of people. I know what it's like to be so different."

Deana and Victor share their needs, their hopes, and what was helpful to them. I talk about the overwhelming sense of responsibility and feeling heavily burdened. Claude nods and talks about how vulnerable and helpless he feels when Sylvia rejects him. Their friends join in and talk about their hurt when Sylvia pushes them away.

Sylvia cries and agrees to let her most loving friends help her. We set up a time frame for people to come and visit. Some folks will take Sylvia out shopping, others will come over and help reorganize the house so Sylvia will be as independent as possible. Everyone agrees to learn how to stand-pivot Sylvia and get her in and out of the car. Holly will teach them. Two of the men are going to come over during the week and take Claude out to dinner while their wives stay with Sylvia. Deana and Victor will keep in touch with Sylvia, and Mary and I will call Claude during the week. We all agree to meet the following week to see what's happened and what's needed.

On the way home Mary and I are excited. We have finally found a way to set up a piece of our support group.

I call Phyllis as soon as I can to tell her what has happened. In her infinite wisdom she says, "You know, David, these kinds of crisis interventions are what we're good at. I think this is the best way for us to be helpful."

When I talk to Phyllis on the phone I realize that her life in Miami continues without me. I'm not sure I like that.

I'm busy with Toughlove even though summertime is not our most active period. I have a conference in California and another in Canada to attend and, as usual, money is critical. I know we all sacrifice to keep Phyllis in Miami but none of us can deny her what she wants so badly.

Every one of Sylvia and Claude's friends shows up for our second meeting. I open the meeting with, "How did the week go?"

"Sylvia was very tired and cried a great deal," they report.

Sylvia speaks up in a quiet voice, "Why isn't it all right for me to grieve?"

"We're afraid of your grief and the losses you have suffered," says a friend.

Everyone cries, including me, as we remember and talk about our experiences.

It's okay to grieve and we're quiet for a while. Then, we check in on our last week's tasks and make new assignments. The people in the group agree to meet on their own and to call if they need help.

Mary and I are pleased. She heads home and I head for Miami with Phyllis's new wheelchair.

PHYLLIS

✳ David's coming back and I can hardly wait. I have so much to show him and love to give him. When he arrives he's brought me my new wheelchair. "David, you look stressed. The lines around your eyes seem deeper. Are you okay?"

"Yes, I'm just tired. I was at a conference in Canada and we had our last session of the support meeting for Sylvia and Claude just before I came here. It's not easy being without you. Phyllis, my dear, you look wonderful. You've lost weight and you look really healthy."

We kiss Jodi and Nitya good-bye and put them on a plane.

DAVID

✳ At the apartment Phyllis shows me one of her new accomplishments. "I'm going swimming." I watch with heartfelt pleasure as she heads out the door, gets on the elevator, wheels to the pool herself. The lifeguard puts Phyllis in the pool and she swims off, showing me her breaststroke, backstroke, and sidestroke. I cheer and applaud.

At the lab Phyllis still struggles to develop leg muscles. She tries so hard that I wish I could do it for her. Instead I encourage her. I become her private cheering section: "Lift! Lift! You can do it, come on. One more, just one more." The anxiety I felt about working alone, our lack of money, and my loneliness evaporates in the Miami sun. Phyllis is really rolling in Dr. Brucker's biofeedback lab. She is up to 40 percent of her back muscles and that has made her swimming so much better.

She has become the unofficial social coordinator of the FES lab. We have dinner with staff and other patients. We go shopping with other couples at the malls.

At Michael and Joyce's home Michael teaches Phyllis to transfer into the car. He's a good teacher and it's obvious to me that her increased strength helps her in every way. Her new wheelchair is more comfortable and allows Phyllis to do much of her own wheeling.

Here in Miami I feel such a part of everything that I hate to leave. I feel lonely already. We greet Meredith at the plane and I kiss Phyllis and Miami good-bye.

PHYLLIS

❋   "Meredith, I'm getting tired of *training* to ride the bike. I'm ready to start riding now."

"Well, go ahead and tell him. I'm sure he'll listen."

So I tell him. "Mark, I can't stay here forever. I have to get back to work. I want to try riding the bike."

"I don't know, Phyllis, you're not strong enough yet. I'm afraid it will just waste your time. You need to be stronger."

Two days later he gives me a stress test on the ergometer and I pass with flying colors. I'm to try the bike at my next appointment, which coincides with David's first day back in Miami.

I'm hooked up to the magic bike, with electrodes on my quads, hamstrings, and gluteals, building my own muscles. The exercise that stops atrophy in its tracks and makes you healthy and aerobic.

I want to sing, "Miami, Miami, what a wonderful town," because of the Miami Project, because of FES, because of biofeedback and Bernard Brucker. It makes my heart sing and pound to be in love with people who believe that my life and their life's work are bound in a worthwhile purpose.

"Come on, Phyllis, you can do it!" yell Jorge and Eduardo, my physical therapists, "push on your own." Go, go ride 'em, cowboy. It's like having a baby. I am on the bike—and all after months of "You may be too fat."

"Oy vay! this is hard."

"Phyllis," my dedicated darling yells, "you can do it! Keep the rhythm!"

And I *can* do it! I can, I can—I am *the little engine that could*! I'm peddling my ass off. Nash kisses me and we are all relieved that I can do it, adipose tissue and all.

Hope, hope—we have been afraid to hope; false hope is a lie we could not tell ourselves so we lived in a kind of despair.

In a way this is another rebirth. A third kind. I am managing to push my body, and besides that I have found real people in wheelchairs living a meaningful life. Businessmen living ordinary lives.

Here I've visited the first person I've ever known who lives in a home that's accessible.

Here I've gotten to know as friends people who are like me.

Michael tutors me. "You won't even notice this after a while. Transfers will be second nature."

Joyce, his wife, is not the wife of a poor cripple but the wife of Michael her equal. He cares for her well.

Michael is a *person*! He can say he'd like to walk, "but not if it means I'd have to lose the last fifteen years."

Although I don't like it, I've learned that I can live without my dearest David for weeks at a time—and so can love him even more.

All these months in Miami have given me physical strength and hope. Not so much hope that I will walk—of course, that is my wish—but real hope in a better future.

Blind faith, faith in God's benevolence and healing, is not my strong suit.

"Jodi, how do you know there is a God?"

"Well, Ma, I can feel God's presence in my life. God is an essence in people," she says.

Mary says that God is the highest aspiration of man. The ideal we aspire to. "Phyllis," she says, "when I ride through the Pennsylvania countryside in the fall and see the gorgeous golds, rust, reds and bronze of the trees against the blue sky, these words from my childhood pop into my head, 'Thank you God for letting me worship in the best of places.' "

Here in Miami at a party, people laugh at my sequined fishtail that Candice made for me.

Yet, there are still nights when my mother floats above my head as I lie in bed. She wears her 1940s blue spring coat over a housedress and apron as though she were in a hurry and had no time to dress, just as she did when I was sick in bed as a child and she'd run out for medicine, lollipops, and books, leaving me alone for a few minutes. Her lovely piano-playing hands reach down to touch me like Michaelangelo's "God Creating Man." I reach up to hold her hand and suddenly, with all the technology of *An American Werewolf in London*, her bones spring through her skin and I am frightened, warned away.

"Phyllis," David commands, "it's time to go home." I know he's right but it takes weeks to let go of Miami and still know I'll be okay.

XXXV

PHYLLIS

✳ Now that I am paralyzed and forced to be still, I lie in bed in early-morning thought, feeling the smell of the cool dewy air of late fall that I have always known.

In New York City the cool smell came with open apartment-house windows, loud voices talking, with TVs and radios tuning up, plumbing sounds and water running, and the sound of feet upon my ceiling. Images of trains summoning people, moving fast; curlers, housecoats, toasters popping, children crying, doors slamming.

In Pennsylvania through open suburban windows, the morning coolness wakes me with the sound of birds close by, geese honking in the distance, squirrels chattering, car doors slamming, lawns being mowed.

I look across the bed and you are there beside me, always. Like the cool spring morning air that follows and surrounds me with familiar pleasure. I love you!

DAVID

※   Phyllis's requests to kill her have been replaced by, "Do you still love me?" Which is quickly followed by, "I know you love me, but I don't know why." Homicide requests are hard to take but easy to answer. Why I love Phyllis is just the reverse, easy to take but hard to answer.

We share a history of thirty-one years, three daughters, and three grandchildren. In the beginning, Phyllis's flamboyant style and gregariousness appealed to me. She seemed to live so much outside of herself. I was her direct opposite. I felt trapped inside my skin. I had no sense of a pathway out or the language to express it. To Phyllis and others I appeared to be a rock. A stable, sturdy force upon which to anchor. An unknowable and unfeeling enigma. The dichotomy of who we were occupied us for at least the first ten years of marriage.

Phyllis: "David, what do you think?" . . . "How do you feel?" . . . "What's going on with you?"

David: "Phyllis, stop embarrassing me." . . . "Do you have to talk to everyone?" . . . "Leave me alone."

Phyllis, my dearest, I love you for forcing me out of myself. For making me grow and take responsibility for becoming a person.

As our early marriage wore on, fought on, we learned to like one another.

Phyllis, my dearest and best friend, I love you for your laughter, your joy, your warmth, your willingness to forgive, your willingness to fight, and your intelligence.

Phyllis's style of thinking is different from mine. I start at beginnings and plod stoically toward ends. Phyllis starts at beginning, middle, and end and quickly moves to end, beginning, and middle. I didn't appreciate how helpful this way of thinking was until we became business partners. I can't work that way and Phyllis can't work my way. Together we enhance each other. Together I am whole.

Phyllis, my dearest, I love and admire your courage.

When you broke your neck you were emotionally and physically devastated. Even through all the ranting, raving, cursing, crying, and sadness you worked hard at becoming better. The tiny steps have produced giant steps.

You get in and out of bed by yourself.

You completely dress and undress without help.

You work and play until your energy runs out.

You reach out to others and bring them hope.

You reach out and create hope for yourself.

Phyllis, you are such a unique and wonderful human, I can't conceive of not loving you.

PHYLLIS

✳ At home, I am lying in bed watching David watch a football game he is enjoying so much. His face is like my own, maybe more familiar.

My darling, I think to myself, there were times early on when I looked into your eyes and they were hard green marbles I could not see past. I was blind and you were hidden.

He watches a play and is virtually playing himself, eyes darting back and forth, teeth clenched, muscles straining. It makes me smile to see his pleasure.

We are old lovers, friends, adventurers, sex partners, parents, playmates, business partners, nurse, and patient and whatever more people can be to each other. We have lived, it seems, three or four lifetimes together. For better, for worse, for richer, for poorer, in sickness and health. And, I love you more through each. This time, I have clung to you for dear life and you have given me the breath of life. I fear, my dearest, that if the shoe were on the other foot, I might not have done as well. You, my darling, put me before your own desires and I finally know that I am loved.